the income tax | root of all evil

By FRANK CHODOROV

introduction by J. BRACKEN LEE

GOVERNOR OF UTAH

THE DEVIN-ADAIR COMPANY

NEW YORK, 1954

To the Memory of
ALBERT J. NOCK

Foreword

THIS WAS, to be sure, "the home of the free and the land of the brave." Americans were free simply because the government was too weak to intervene in the private affairs of the people—it did not have the money to do so—and they were brave because a free people is always venturesome. The obligation of freedom is a willingness to stand on your own feet.

The early American wanted it that way. He was wary of government, especially one that was out of his reach. He had just rid himself of far-away and self-sufficient political establishment and he was not going to tolerate anything like it in his newly founded country. He recognized the need of some sort of government, to keep order, to protect him in the exercise of his rights, and to look after his interests in foreign lands. But, he wanted it understood that the powers of that government would be clearly defined and be limited; it could not go beyond specified limits. It was in recognition of this fear of centralized power that the Founding Fathers put into the Constitution—it never would have been ratified without them—very specific restraints on the federal government.

In other matters, the early American was willing to put his faith in home government, in a government of neighbors, in a government that one could keep one's eyes on and, if necessary, lay one's hands on. For that reason, the United States was founded as a Union of separate and autonomous commonwealths. The states could go in for any political experiments the folks might want to try out—even socialism, for that matter—but the federal government had no such leeway. After all, there were other states nearby, and if a citizen did not like the way one state government was managing its affairs, he could move across the border; that threat of competition would keep each state from going too far in making changes or in intervening in the lives of the citizens.

The Constitution, then, kept the federal government off balance and weak. And a weak government is the corollary of a strong people.

The Sixteenth Amendment changed all that. In the first place, by enabling the federal government to put its hands into the pockets and pay envelopes of the people, it drew their allegiance away from their local governments. It made them citizens of the United States rather than of their respective states. Their loyalty followed their money, which was now taken from them not by their local representatives, over whom they had some control, but by the representatives of the other forty-seven states. They became subject to the will of the central government, and their state of subjection was emphasized by every increase in the income-tax levies.

The state governments likewise lost more and more of their autonomy. Not only was their source of revenue being dried up by federal preemption, so that they had less and less for the social services a government should provide, but they were compelled in their extremity to apply to the central authorities for help. In so doing they necessarily gave up some of their independence. They found it difficult to stand up to the institution from which they had to beg grants-in-aid. Furthermore, the federal government was in position to demand subservience from the state governments as a condition for subventions. It has now become politically wise for governors, legislators, and Congressmen to "play ball" with the central government; they have been reduced to being procurement officers for the citizens who elect them. The economic power which the federal government secured by the Sixteenth Amendment enabled it to bribe the state governments, as well as the citizens, into submission to its will.

In that way, the whole spirit of the Union and of its Constitution has been liquidated. Income taxation has made of the United States as completely centralized a nation as any that went before it; the very kind of establishment the Founding Fathers abhorred was set up by this simple change in the tax laws. This is no longer the "home of the free," and what bravery remains is traceable to a tradition that is fast losing ground.

For those of us who still believe that freedom is best, the way is clear: we must concentrate on the correction of the mistake of 1913. The Sixteenth Amendment must be repealed. Nothing less will do. For it is only because it has this enormous revenue that the federal government is able to institute procedures that violate the individual's right to himself and his property; enforcement agencies must be paid. With the repeal of the amendment, the socialistic measures visited upon us these past thirty years will vanish.

The purchase of elections with federal money will no longer be possible. And the power and dignity of the home governments will be restored.

This measure should be supported by the governors and legislators of all the states. Every state in the Union now contributes in income taxes to the federal government more than it gets back in grants-in-aid; this is inevitable, because the cost of maintaining the huge federal machinery must come out of the taxes before the citizen can get anything. With the abolition of income taxation the states will be better able to serve its citizens, and because the state governments are closer and more responsive to the will of the people, there is greater chance that the citizens will get their full dollar's worth in services.

However, the principal argument for the repeal of the Sixteenth Amendment is that only in that way can freedom from an interventionist government be restored to the American people.

J. BRACKEN LEE,
Governor of Utah

Argument

Tradition has a way of hanging on even after it is, for all practical purposes, dead. We in this country still use individualistic terms—as, for instance, the rights of man—when, as a matter of fact, we think and behave in the framework of collectivistic doctrine. We support and advocate such practices as farm-support prices, social security, government housing, socialized medicine, conscription, and all sorts of ideas that stem from the thesis that man has no rights except those given him by government.

Despite this growing tendency to look to political power as the source of material betterment and as the guide to our personal destinies, we still talk of limited government, states' rights, checks and balances, and of the personal virtues of thrift, industry, and initiative. Thanks to our literature, the tradition hangs on even though it has lost force.

But there are many Americans to whom the new trend is distasteful, partly because they are traditionalists, partly because they find it personally unpleasant, partly because reason tells that it must lead to the complete subjugation of the individual, as in Nazi Germany or Communist Russia, and they don't like the prospect. It is for these Americans that this book was written. For their opposition to the trend takes the shape of reform, while nothing will turn it but revolution. And by "revolution" I mean the return to the people of that sovereignty which our tradition assumes them to have. I mean the return to them of the power which government confiscated by way of the Sixteenth Amendment.

When you examine any species of government intervention you find that it is made possible by revenues. A government is as strong as its income. Contrariwise, the independence of the people is in direct proportion to the amount of their wealth they can enjoy. We cannot restore traditional American freedom unless we limit the government's power to tax. No tinkering with this, that, or the other law will stop the trend toward socialism. We must repeal the Sixteenth Amendment.

Washington, D.C.   F. C.
February 1954

Contents

CHAPTER I

Solomon's Yoke

It is told—1 Kings, Chapter 12—that the people of Israel petitioned their new king, Rehoboam, son of Solomon, to relieve them of the "yoke" his father had suffered them to bear. The "yoke," we learn from the story, was the cost of maintaining the political establishment; it was an income tax.

The designation of a levy on one's production as a "yoke" is interesting; it shows how keen is the mind unencumbered with erudition. The yoke symbolizes the beast of burden, who, of course, has no right of property. When the human is similarly deprived of what he has produced—which is the essence of income taxation—he is indeed degraded to the status of an ox. The Israelite, who maintained that he was made in the image of God, sensed the indignity; he wanted none of the "yoke."

The story goes on to say that Rehoboam promised to take his subjects' plea under advisement. Apparently, he talked the matter over with his ministers. What they said to him is unrecorded, but we can infer from his ultimate decision that they strongly advised him against any reduction of the income tax; after all, ministers have to be supported in the style to which bureaucrats always like to be accustomed. So, after shilly-shallying for three days, Rehoboam came to

1

the point and said: "Whereas my father did lade you with a heavy yoke, I will add to your yoke: my father did chastise you with whips, but I will chastise you with scorpions."

Whatever chastisement with scorpions may be, it is certainly not pleasant to the recipient. And that is something you might remember when an agent of the Internal Revenue Department calls you on the carpet for not including in your income-tax return the winnings you made at poker or the gratuities you received as a waiter or a beautician. Things could be much worse with us than they are; we could be chastised with scorpions.

We learn from this biblical story that income taxation is a very old custom. Antiquarians find mention of the practice in the annals of Egypt, as far back as 1580 B.C. In those days, it appears, the Grand Vizier did not levy on the incomes of his subjects but on the incomes of public officials; since the latter had nothing of their own to tax—public officials are not producers—their taxable funds consisted of what they had mulcted from the producing public. It was tax farming. There is something to be said in favor of that system. Since the tax collector gets his "cut" first, before turning over the balance to the central government, he can never be accused of accepting bribes—a charge that is sometimes levied against agents of our Internal Revenue Bureau.

Even evasion of the income tax, by way of false income-tax returns, is not a modern invention. Gibbon makes mention of the use of racks and scourges in ancient Rome, up to the fourth century of the Christian era, to get the truth out of suspected evaders. We have not, at any rate, come to that, although we do on occasions cast a tax dodger into durance vile.

For something really different and quite startling in the income-tax business, we must again refer to the biblical story. Some of the Israelites were so resentful about the "yoke" that when Rehoboam's chief tax collector, one called Hadoram, made his round among them, they unceremoniously met him with such a hail of stones "that he died." This was rather hard on Hadoram and his family, and is not to be recommended for agents of the Internal Revenue Bureau. In the latter part of this book—which concerns itself with the *immorality* of the income tax—a more orderly and effective way of getting rid of the "yoke" that Americans have been suffered to wear since 1913 will be suggested. Provided, of course, they want to get rid of it; provided they have the sense of self-respect and human dignity that characterized those stone-throwing Israelites.

CHAPTER II

Politically Speaking, What Is "Evil"?

THE SUBTITLE of this book is "Root of All Evil."

If there is an "evil" there must be a "good"—for the one is the opposite of the other. Hence, we must define "good" in order to establish the fact that an "evil" exists or threatens. It is not necessary to prove that the "good" is really good for all peoples at all times and under all circumstances—in short, that it is made in Heaven. Something can be said for that thesis, but this book—which deals with the income tax and its effects on our social, economic, and political life—is not concerned with it. For the purpose of this book, it is only necessary that we agree on a definition of "good" so that we can recognize its opposite.

Thus, the Judeo=Christian tradition holds that in the field of morals all that is "good" is set down in the Ten Commandments, and that practices running counter to these dicta are "evil." There have been civilizations in which such practices as adultery, thievery, and even murder were looked upon as in the regular order of things, neither reprehensible nor praiseworthy, and in these civilizations the Ten Commandments, if known, would carry no weight. We can argue that our moral code makes for better living and is therefore superior to whatever went for a moral code in these primi-

4

tive civilizations. That may be so. The point is that the Ten Commandments, though written in Heaven, had to be understood and accepted on earth before we could measure "good" and "evil."

In the American political tradition, which claims kinship with Judeo-Christian morality, all is "evil" that violates the doctrine of natural rights, as set down in the Declaration of Independence. We are agreed on that. We are also agreed—if we accept the tradition—that the source of these rights is God; which is simply an admission that we have scratched our heads for some other explanation of these rights and, having found none, have taken recourse to "the nature of things." The American tradition rests its case squarely on the premise that the human being is endowed with rights by his very existence; that is what makes him human. Hence, any political action which attempts to violate these rights violates his human-ness, and thus becomes "evil." Putting it another way, any political action which disregards man's inalienable rights disregards God.

The Constitution of the United States is a manmade instrument; it has no other sanction. Yet it has won acceptance with Americans as the yardstick of political "good," because it was conceived as a practical instrument for the prevention of transgressions of our rights, either by the government or by citizens. Over the years, the Constitution has come to be looked upon as the guardian angel of these rights. When an American asserts that a law or official act is in his opinion "unconstitutional"—even if the Supreme Court has not so adjudicated—he may or may not have the letter of the Constitution in mind; more likely, his judgment

5

is based on what he knows of the spirit of the instrument. Surely, an amendment of the Constitution cannot be said to be "unconstitutional"; yet, if the amendment seems to be violative of the original purpose of the Constitution, the citizen does not hesitate so to describe it. A case in point was the Eighteenth Amendment which, for the thirteen years it was in effect, was decried because it gave the government power to control the drinking habits of the citizen; his rights were invaded.

The Constitution, then, is held in high esteem only because of the high esteem Americans put upon the doctrine of natural rights. Any law, political practice, or even amendment that infringes those rights is automatically deemed "unconstitutional." The infringement is "evil."

With this definition of "evil" in mind, it is the purpose of this book to show that many laws and governmental practices are impregnated with it, and to trace this wholesale infringement of our rights to the power acquired by the federal government in 1913 to tax our incomes—the Sixteenth Amendment. That is the "root." Furthermore, proof will be offered to support the proposition that the "evil" has reached the point where the doctrine of natural rights has been all but abrogated in fact, if not in theory.

As a consequence, the kind of government we are acquiring is distinctly different from that envisaged by the Founding Fathers; it is fast becoming a government that conceives itself to be the source of rights, which it gives and can recall at its own pleasure. The transformation is not yet complete, but it will be seen as we go along that completion is not far off—if nothing is done to prevent it.

6

Whether anything will be done to stop the "unconstitutional" trend depends on how far the "evil" has penetrated the consciousness of the American people. An evil is not only something that is done to us; more often, it is something we do to ourselves, consciously or by way of weakness. A drunkard may acquire his bad habit from his associates or he may bring it on without outside influence.

In the case of the practices resulting from income taxation, it will be shown that most of them are demanded or supported by large segments of society; the government merely compounds the evil. *A people who are intent on getting something-for-nothing from government cannot cavil over the infringement of their rights by that government;* in fact, if the price demanded for the gratuities is the relinquishment of rights, they are not averse to paying it. There is evidence enough that this trade is often made, and that the government is able to enter into it because of its income-tax revenues.

When an "evil" becomes customary, it tends to lose the negative value put on it and in men's minds tends to become a "good." And so, we hear much these days in praise of the very kind of government which the Founding Fathers tried to prevent by their blueprint; that is, of a paternalistic establishment ruling for and over a subject people. *A virtue has been made of what was once considered a vice.* This transmutation of political values has been accompanied by a transmutation of moral values, as a matter of necessity; people who have no rights are presumably without free will; at least, there is no call for the exercise of free will (as in the case of a slave) when a paternalistic government assumes the obligations of living.

7

Why, for instance, should one be charitable when the government provides for the incompetent or the unfortunate? Why should one be honest when all that is necessary to "get by" is to obey the law? Why should one give thought to one's future when the matter can be left to a munificent government? And, with the government providing "free" schooling, including "free" lunches, even the parents' obligations to their children can be sloughed off.

Thus, the fabric of Judeo-Christian morality is undergoing deterioration as a result of the "evil" that has infiltrated our political life. That government has become more corrupt is only incidental to this general deterioration; things being as they are, our attitude toward such corruption must undergo a change: *the mortal sin becomes a venial sin under the force of custom.* Nor can the Ten Commandments hold up under the transformation of our political and social attitudes, for a people who are denied rights, or who relinquish their claim to rights, are likely to put little worth on personality.

This treatise on the Sixteenth Amendment will proceed under these general lines:

That as a consequence of this law our government is being transformed into one alien to the American tradition.

That social and individual values are likewise undergoing transmutation.

That, in short, America is no longer the America of the Declaration of Independence.

Finally, and most important, we shall suggest a means for reversing the trend and restoring the "good" of our tradition.

8

CHAPTER III

Yours Is Not Your Own

THERE ARE taxes and taxes. All are alike in two respects: they are compulsory and they are part of production. "Taxation," says the *Encyclopedia Britannica,* is "that part of the revenue of the State which is obtained by compulsory dues and charges upon its subjects."

Nevertheless, the "compulsory dues and charges" are usually divided into two major categories: direct and indirect. The reason for the classification is the method of collection; but the effect of direct taxes on public affairs makes them different in kind.

Indirect taxes are so called because the government does not get them directly from the payer; they are collected for the government by manufacturers and merchants, who recoup their outlay from their customers in the price of goods and services. *All indirect taxes are added to price.*

The most important of these indirect taxes are tariffs and excise levies. Tariffs are paid by the importer, who transfers the charge to his customer, who in turn adds the cost to the price he charges the next processor, and so on down until the ultimate consumer absorbs the original importer's outlay, plus all the profits that have accrued to each handler. Excise taxes, like those paid on tobacco and liquor, are collected through the sale of stamps and licenses. Sales taxes are likewise found in the price of goods.

Indirect taxes are mere money raisers; there is nothing in the character of these taxes that involves any other purpose. In levying them, the government does not call on any principle other than that the citizen must pay for the upkeep of his government, in proportion to the amount of goods he consumes. It is as if the government were saying to the citizen: "Sorry, old man, but we need money with which to carry on this political establishment, and we don't have any other source of money but you; we will, however, ease the pain of payment by hiding these taxes in the price of the goods you buy." The government does not question the right of the citizen to his property. The citizen need not pay these taxes; he can go without.

This alternative does not apply to direct taxes. The principal direct taxes are those levied on inheritances and incomes. (Another is the tax on land values, which we shall disregard because it has no bearing on the thesis of this book.) Except for payroll deductions, which is a device employed by government for the easy and certain collection of taxes on wages, direct taxes are paid directly to the government. They are not charged against the consumer in price, although, as we shall see later, they affect his standard of living even more materially.

Income and inheritance taxes imply the denial of private property, and in that are different in principle from all other taxes.

10

YOURS IS NOT YOUR OWN

The government says to the citizen: "Your earnings are not exclusively your own; we have a claim on them, and our claim precedes yours; we will allow you to keep some of it, because we recognize your need, not your right; but whatever we grant you for yourself is for us to decide."

This is no exaggeration. Take a look at the income-tax report that you are required by law to make out, and you will see that the government arbitrarily sets down the amount of your income you may have for your living, for your business requirements, for the maintenance of your family, for medical expenses, and so on. After granting these exemptions, with a flourish of generosity, the government decides what percentage of the remainder it will appropriate. The rest you may have.

The percentage of the appropriation may be (and has been) raised from year to year, and the exemptions may be (and have been) lowered from year to year.* The amount of your earnings that you may retain for yourself is determined by the needs of government, and you have nothing to say about it. The right of decision as to the disposition of your property rests in the government by virtue of the Sixteenth Amendment of the Constitution, which reads as follows:

"The Congress shall have power to lay and collect taxes on incomes, from whatever source derived, without appor-

* In 1913, a single person, not entitled to any exemptions for dependencies or anything else, paid a tax of $20 on an income of $5000. A person similarly situated in 1951 paid $964. The comparison is even more striking when the purchasing power of the dollar in the two years is taken into consideration.

11

tionment among the several states, and without regard to any census or enumeration."*

The amendment puts no limit on governmental confiscation. The government can, under the law, take everything the citizen earns, even to the extent of depriving him of all above mere subsistence, which it must allow him in order that he may produce something to be confiscated. Whichever way you turn this amendment, you come up with the fact that it gives the government a prior lien on all the property produced by its subjects.

In short, when this amendment became part of the Constitution, in 1913, the absolute right of property in the United States was violated.

That, of course, is the essence of socialism. Whatever else socialism is, or is claimed to be, its first tenet is the denial of private property. All brands of socialism, and there are many, are agreed that property rights must be vested in the political establishment. None of the schemes that are identified with this ideology, such as the nationalization of industry, or socialized medicine, or the abolition of free choice, or the planned economy, can become operative if the individual's claim to his property is recognized by the

---

* The apportionment of taxes among the states according to population was originally put into the Constitution in order to prevent a combination of states from forcing through a levy that would hit the more opulent states harder than themselves. Also, it prevented the more populous states from raiding the citizens of the sparsely settled states. In both instances, this provision compelled the levying of taxes on individuals equally, according to their consumption, and prevented the levying on citizens according to their wealth or, for that matter, according to their religion, political affiliations, or other personal identification. This provision was a bar to the introduction of the income tax.

12

government. It is for that reason that *all socialists, beginning with Karl Marx, have advocated income taxation, the heavier the better.*°

So then, when the Sixteenth Amendment became part of the Constitution, the American political order, which rested on the axiom of inalienable rights, underwent a major operation. The great debate in the Constitutional Convention of 1789 was over the question as to whether this country should have a republican or democratic form of government; the question was finally resolved in 1913, when the door was opened for the introduction of the socialistic form.

As our inquiry leads us to consider the institutions that have become fixed in the American pattern, we see how far America has gone along the road of socialism. We shall also see that many institutions, such as states' rights and free enterprise, that were long considered peculiar to our political and social order, have lost value with the American citizen. Even the abhorrence attached to the word "socialism" in this country before 1913 is wearing off, and an increasing number of the citizenry (perhaps the majority) use it as the symbol of a great ideal. All these changes in our culture are directly traceable to the abandonment of the doctrine of private property—that is, to the Sixteenth Amendment.

So long as the confiscation of private property is legalized, this country is not immune to the advent of ultimate socialism, which is communism.

The basic tenet of communism is the vesting of all prop-

° Progressive income and inheritance taxation was first advocated as a means of destroying private property by Karl Marx, in the *Communist Manifesto,* published in 1848. Thereafter, every socialist party platform included this plank.

erty rights in the state. Already nearly one third of our national income is being taxed away from us.° One or two more national "emergencies" can well bring about the confiscation of the other two thirds, and thus effect the final transition to communism. We could slither into it quite without being aware of it.

Any effort to reverse the trend must begin with the reestablishment in the American culture of the inviolability of private property. If Americans were again to put that right at the pinnacle of their values, the repeal of the Sixteenth Amendment would follow as a matter of course. Therefore, it is necessary that we digress in this inquiry for a moment to consider the philosophic support of the axiom—that *the individual has an inalienable right to his property.*

Even a thief will justify his way of life. The human being must have a moral code of some kind to ease the difficulty of living with himself. And there is no difficulty in making up a code to fit any given condition, language being as rich as it is, if one hits on an axiom as a basis; an axiom needs no proof.

° This estimate is based on figures published by the United States Treasury. It includes local, state, and federal taxes. Exactness of computation is made difficult by the method of arriving at the "national income." The government figure includes income of all kinds, that earned by the worker or the corporation and that paid to the government official. The latter's salary is of course paid out of taxes taken from producers and is therefore a duplication. This is the same as computing the family's income by adding to the breadwinner's wages the amount he gives his wife for household expenses. The official "national income" includes the subsidies paid to the farmer and the taxes paid by the farmer to make these subsidies possible. If government handouts and government salaries were deducted from this official figure, and only income from production were included, the "national income" would be far less than the official figure, and the percentage taken by taxes would be greater.

14

The axiom of socialism is that the individual has no inherent rights. The privileges and prerogatives that the individual enjoys are grants from society, acting through its management committee, the government. That is the condition the individual must accept for the benefit of being a member of society. Hence, the socialists (including many who do not so name themselves) reject the statement of rights in the Declaration of Independence, calling it a fiction of the eighteenth century.

In support of his denial of natural rights, the socialist points out that there is no positive proof in favor of that doctrine. Where is the documentary evidence? Did God hand man a signed statement endowing him with the rights he claims for himself, but denies to the birds and beasts who also inhabit the earth? If in answer to these questions you bring in the soul idea, you are right back to where you were in the beginning: how can you prove that man has a soul?

Those who accept the axiom of natural rights are backed against the wall by that kind of reasoning, until they examine the opposite axiom, that all rights are grants or loans from government. *Where did government get the rights which it dispenses?* If it is said that its fund of rights is collected from individuals, as the condition for their membership in society, the question arises, where did the individual get the rights that he gave up? He cannot give up what he never had in the first place, which is what the socialist maintains.

What is this thing called government, which can grant and take away rights? There are all sorts of answers to that question, but all the answers will agree on one point, that

15

government is a social instrument enjoying a monopoly of coercion. The socialist says that the monopoly of coercion is vested in the government in order that it may bring about an ideal social and economic order; others say that the government must have a monopoly of coercion in order to prevent individuals from using coercion on one another. In short, the essential characteristic of government is power. If, then, we say that our rights stem from government, on a loan basis, we admit that whoever gets control of the power vested in government is the author of rights. And simply because he has the power to enforce his will. Thus, *the basic axiom of socialism, in all its forms, is that might is right.*

And that means that power is all there is to morality. If I am bigger and stronger than you, and you have no way of defending yourself, then it is right if I thrash you; the fact that I did thrash you is proof that I had the right to do so. On the other hand, if you can intimidate me with a gun, then right returns to your side. All of which comes to mere nonsense. And a social order based on the socialistic axiom— which makes the government the final judge of all morality— is a nonsensical society. It is a society in which the highest value is the acquisition of power—as exemplified in a Hitler or a Stalin—and the fate of those who cannot acquire it is subservience as a condition of existence.

The senselessness of the socialistic axiom is that there would be no society, and therefore no government, if there were no individuals. The human being is the unit of all social institutions; without a man there cannot be a crowd. Hence, we are compelled to look to the individual to find

16

an axiom on which to build a nonsocialistic moral code. What does he tell us about himself?

In the first place, he tells us that above all things he wants to live. He tells us this even when he first comes into this world and lets out a yell. Because of that primordial desire, he maintains, he has a right to live. Certainly, nobody else can establish a valid claim to his life, and for that reason he traces his own title to an authority that transcends all men, to God. That title makes sense.

When the individual says he has a valid title to life, he means that all that is he, is his own; his body, his mind, his faculties. Maybe there is something else to life, such as a soul, but without going into that realm, he is willing to settle on what he knows about himself—his consciousness. All that is "I" is "mine." That implies, of course, that all that is "you" is "yours"—for, every "you" is an "I." Rights work both ways.

But, while just wanting to live gives the individual a title to life, it is an empty title unless he can acquire the things that make life livable, beginning with food, raiment, and shelter. These things do not come to you because you want them; they come as the result of putting labor to raw materials. You have to give something of yourself—your brawn or your brain—to make the necessary things available. Even wild berries have to be picked before they can be eaten. But the energy you put out to make the necessary things is part of you; it *is* you. *Therefore, when you cause these things to exist, your title to yourself, your labor, is extended to the things. You have a right to them simply because you have a right to life.*

That is the moral basis of the right of property. "I own

17

it because I made it" is a title that proves itself. The recognition of that title is implied in the statement that "I *make* so many dollars a week." That is literally true.

But what do you mean when you say you own the thing you produced? Say it is a bushel of wheat. You produced it to satisfy your desire for bread. You can grind the wheat into flour, bake the loaf of bread, eat it, or share it with your family or a friend. Or you give part of the wheat to the miller in payment for his labor; the part you give him, in the form of wages, is his because he gave you labor in exchange. Or you sell half the bushel of wheat for money, which you exchange for butter, to go with· the bread. Or you put the money in the bank so that you can have something else later on, when you want it.

In other words, your ownership entitles you to use your judgment as to what you will do with the product of your labor—consume it, give it away, sell it, save it. Freedom of disposition is the substance of property rights.

Interference with this freedom of disposition is, in the final analysis, interference with your right to life. At least, that is your reaction to such interference, for you describe such interference with a word that expresses a deep emotion: you call it "robbery." What's more, if you find that this robbery persists, if you are regularly deprived of the fruits of your labor, you lose interest in laboring. The only reason you work is to satisfy your desires, and if experience shows that despite your efforts your desires go unsatisfied, you become stingy about laboring. You become a "poor" producer.

Suppose the freedom of disposition is taken away from you entirely. That is, you become a slave; you have no right

18

of property. Whatever you produce is taken by somebody else, and though a good part of it is returned to you, in the way of sustenance, medical care, housing, you cannot under the law dispose of your output; if you try to, you become the legal "robber." Your concern in production wanes and you develop an attitude toward laboring that is called 'a "slave" psychology. Your interest in yourself also drops because you sense that without the right of property you are not much different from the other living things in the barn. The clergyman may tell you you are a man, with a soul, but you sense that without the right of property you are somewhat less of a man than the one who can dispose of your production as he wills. If you are a human, how human are you?

It is silly, then, to prate of human rights being superior to property rights, because the right of ownership is traceable to the right to life, which is certainly inherent in the human being. Property rights are in fact human rights.

A society built around the denial of this fact is, or must become, a slave society—although the socialists describe it differently. It is a society in which some produce and others dispose of their output. The laborer is not stimulated by the prospect of satisfying his desires but by fear of punishment. When his ownership is not interfered with, when he works for himself, he is inclined to develop his faculties of production, because he has unlimited desires. He works for food, as a matter of necessity, but when he has a sufficiency of food he begins to think of fancy dishes, a tablecloth, and music with his meals. There is no end of desires the human being can conjure up, and will work for, provided he feels reasonably sure that his labor will not be in

19

vain. Contrariwise, when the law deprives him of the incentive of enjoyment, he will work only as necessity compels him. What use is there in putting out more effort?

Therefore, the general production of a socialistic society must tend to decline to the point of mere subsistence.

The economic decline of a society without property rights is followed by the loss of other values. It is only when we have a sufficiency of necessaries that we give thought to nonmaterial things, to what is called culture. On the other hand, we find we can do without books, or even moving pictures, when existence is at stake. Even more than that, we who have no right to own certainly have no right to give, and charity becomes an empty word; in a socialistic order, no one need give thought to an unfortunate neighbor, because it is the duty of the government, the only property owner, to take care of him; it might even become a crime to give a "bum" a dime. When the denial of the right of the individual is negated through the denial of ownership, the sense of personal pride, which distinguishes man from beast, must decay from disuse.

The income tax is not only a tax; it is an instrument that has the potentiality of destroying a society of humans.

CHAPTER IV

How It Came Upon Us

THE CONSTITUTION of 1789 barred the income tax. The Fathers could not have put it in, even if they had a mind to, and there is no evidence that they had. A century later, when Americans were flirting with this invasion of property rights, legal minds tried to twist the language of the Constitution to their support. Whatever crumbs of comfort they got out of word juggling, the fact is that the Americans of 1789 would have none of this income tax. They were not that kind of people.

Behind these people lay a century and a half of training for freedom. Individualism—which is nothing but a high regard for oneself—had been beaten into their souls; their conquest of nature had taught them the lessons of self-reliance and self-respect. When it was necessary to wage war in defense of the freedom they had wrung from the wilderness, they were well prepared, not materially, but spiritually. John Adams, writing in 1818, said: "the Revolution was in the hearts of men"... it was effected "before the war commenced." They had come by freedom the hard way and they meant to hold on to it.

In point of fact, they went to war with King George III over what we might deem trifles. When you compare the disabilities put on the Americans by the British Crown, as listed in the Declaration of Independence, with what other peoples have complacently suffered from governments, you recognize the high price these Americans put on freedom. How petty the indictment of George reads when one thinks of what the Germans endured under Hitler, the Russians under Stalin! And if we could penetrate our own adjustment to bureaucratic interference, and could see things as they really are, we would write a new Declaration that would make Jefferson's sound picayune.

One of the principal causes of the Resolution was taxation. The Americans summed up their attitude toward taxation in the slogan "Taxation without representation is tyranny." The fact is, they looked upon taxation as a form of tyranny, or an invasion of their property rights, with or without representation, but were willing to make some sort of compromise with it as a matter of necessity; the compromise was "representation." Judging by their reluctance to suffer taxes imposed by their own governments, local or state, it is a certainty that if the Crown had given them representation in Parliament they would have disliked taxes only a little less. The levies laid upon them by the Crown were so minuscule, compared to those their progeny have learned to endure, that the fuss they made seems ridiculous. It seems ridiculous only because we are a different kind of people.

As for an income tax, there would never have been a Revolution if the Americans of 1776 had had any notion of offering it to King George. They probably could have had representation in both houses of Parliament in exchange for such a boon; he would have given them any other kind of "freedom" their hearts desired. But a people who remonstrated so vigorously over a measly tea tax could hardly have understood the idea of letting their pockets be picked. The suggestion would have sounded preposterous.

The Constitution did not give Americans freedom; they had been free long before it was written, and when it was put up for ratification they eyed it suspiciously, lest it infringe their freedom. The Federalists, the advocates of ratification, went to great pains to assure the people that under the Constitution they would be just as free as they ever were. Madison, in particular, stressed the point that there would be no change in their personal status in the new setup, that *the contemplated government would simply be the foreign department of the several states.* The Constitution itself is a testimonial to the temper of the times, for it fashioned a government so restricted in its powers as to prevent any infraction of freedom; that was the reason for the famous "checks and balances." Any other kind of constitution could not have got by.

In the important matter of taxation, the Constitution quite definitely granted the new government very limited powers: import tariffs and excise taxes. Even the latter were grudgingly admitted. The only federal taxing powers on which there was general agreement were tariffs; the "infant industry" argument—the need of encouraging manufactures in the new country by protection from foreign competition— carried weight with the people, and it was conceded that a federal monopoly of tariffs would be better than different tariffs by the thirteen states. Hamilton, however, pleaded (in *The Federalist Papers*) the inadequacy of income from tariffs alone. He had in mind not only the expected expenses of the new government, and the need of establishing its credit position, but also the funding and paying off of the Continental debts. He asked for the privilege of sharing internal taxes with the states. He specifically rejected the idea of income taxation, both because it would yield little and because it would be repulsive to the people.

And so, the government of the United States got along with what it could get out of tariffs and a few excise taxes until the Civil War; it is interesting to note that the excise levies were dropped in 1817, and not restored until the Civil War. As a consequence, it was a weak government, in the sense that it could not become bothersome; and the freedom of the people made them strong, so that wealth multiplied and the country flourished. The government did lead the nation into two stupid wars, but these were cut short mainly by lack of funds; the national credit, thanks to low taxes, was weak and federal borrowing was extremely limited. Under the doctrine of eminent domain, the government did create a privileged class—which it always does when it steps into the economic picture—by handing out land grants.

But, on the whole, previous to the Civil War the government of the United States confined itself to the business for which it was created, that of protecting people in the enjoyment of their God-given rights. It should not be forgotten that the Founding Fathers, agreeing with John Locke, with whose writings they were familiar, thought of government principally as *an instrument for safeguarding private property;* and that was considered the prime business of the United States government until 1860.

24

In 1862, Lincoln instituted the first income-tax law in American history. The debate in Congress over this major change in our fiscal policy makes curious reading. It was tacitly agreed that the law was unconstitutional, because it was a direct tax. A few Congressmen tried to stick the "excise" label on the proposed tax, thus forcing it into the formula of the Constitution. But, on the whole, the argument for it rested on the need for money to carry on the war. It was a matter of expediency only. The Constitution was set aside.

That is as it should be. If there is any moral justification for war, it is the need of safeguarding the life of the community. When the existence of the nation is at stake, the natural inclination of a people is to suspend their claim to rights. Their lives are forfeit in the common cause, and so should be their property. The only practical way for putting the property of the people to the common effort is to confiscate it, and income taxation is the perfect confiscatory instrument. But, since defense of the homeland is in the interests of all, both necessity and equity demand that there should be no discrimination and no limit: all that is needed should be taken without regard to rights, even as life is conscripted. It is everybody's house that is on fire, and every available water bucket, without regard to ownership, must be taken to put out the conflagration. So, if war is justified, unlimited and unrestrained income taxation can also be justified. The question is: when is war justified?

Every war is fought with current wealth. There is no way of shooting off cannons that have not yet been made, no way of feeding soldiers with the produce of the next generation.

25

The argument that a future generation can be made to pay the costs of a present war is both specious and deceptive; it cannot be done. All the labor and all the materials expended in the struggle are current, not future, labor and materials. *We pay as we fight.*

The deception that some of the costs may be put on the future is created so as to ease the strain that total confiscation would put on patriotism. To prevent dissatisfaction with the war from getting out of hand, the government takes what it needs, and gives I.O.U.'s (bonds) to the owner. But, this I.O.U. is not payment for the goods taken; it is a claim on future production. So that, the holder of the I.O.U., the grandson of the one whose goods were taken for the war, can demand from other grandsons a share of their production. *The bondholder is simply a partner of the tax collector.* But how is this payment for a past war?

It has been argued that if the government could not borrow it could not wage war. This may be true; neither could it wage war without soldiers. But if people will not give up their property or risk their lives, then the war is not wanted. If the war is not wanted, why should it be waged? If, instead of resorting to loans, the government should confiscate whatever it needs for the purpose, perhaps a waning patriotism would cause the war to be called off.

Those who describe bonds as payment for past years are wont to overlook the fact that the bonds, taken as a whole, are never paid up. The bonded debt of a nation has a way of increasing from generation to generation. That is so because each generation, or its government, encounters a new emergency that needs financing, and it is most convenient to say that the next generation ought to pay for the benefits it will derive from meeting the present emergency. But every generation conveniently ignores the obligation it has inherited. And so the national debt grows.

Since all bonds are claims on production, what really happens when bonds are issued is—let's call it by its right name—counterfeiting; the amount of purchasing power, or money, is increased.

There are several ways by which bonds are monetized, but that is not germane to the present subject; the point is that all bonds add to the fund of money in circulation, and unless the additional money is accompanied by an additional amount of goods in the market, we have inflation. Inflation is simply a greater amount of money bidding for the same amount of goods. The dollar looks like the old dollar, but it buys less. Hence, even the bond buyers are eventually cheated. The dollars they put into the bonds could have bought them more goods than the dollars they earn after the bonds have been issued, or the dollars they get from the government when the bonds mature. It takes a violent wrench of logic to say that we pay for past wars by depreciating the value of the dollar.

Government borrows on its ability to tax, because taxes are its only source of revenue, the only security it has to offer the lender.

Thanks to its low taxing power, the Lincoln administration had difficulty in disposing an issue of bonds bearing twelve percent interest. That means that its credit was very poor, and it had to resort to confiscation. Its first income-tax law called for a flat three percent of net income over $600 a year; this was quite an exemption in itself, since at that time a man could buy an all-wool suit of clothes for $6. The method of collection was simplicity itself: the citizen declared his income on his own estimate, unchecked, and his estimate was published in the newspapers, the idea being that public opinion would compel a degree of honesty.

However, the amount brought in by this tax was not enough to carry on the war, and within two years Lincoln got around to the graduated income tax. Thus was brought into our fiscal policy the *ability-to-pay* doctrine. This doctrine, new at the time, has since attained the dignity of an axiom of taxation. Yet, when we examine it under the light of ethics it does not shine so well; and it is a complete denial of the equality principle that guided the Fathers in establishing the Republic. The taxing power of the federal government was thus limited in the Constitution:

> "No capitation, or other direct, Tax shall be laid, unless in Proportion to the Census or Enumeration herein before directed to be taken."

There is no tax that can be more properly described as "direct" than an income tax. In order to get around this prohibition in the Constitution, the Lincoln administration arbitrarily declared its income levy an "excise" tax, and the Supreme Court upheld this perversion of language in a decision rendered in 1868; showing that the art of proving a point by changing a definition was practiced long before the discovery of the modern "science" of semantics.

Reinforcing the prohibition of a direct tax is the requirement that taxes shall be levied in proportion to the population. The meaning is clear: that in respect to the law all citizens are to be considered equal, as persons, and should be taxed accordingly; their possessions have nothing to do with their legal status. A man who has acquired (presumably by honest methods) a large amount of wealth is legally on a par with the one less fortunate or less proficient. The dictum that "all men are created free and equal" held in the matter of taxes as it did in the matter of social stratification; the Constitution recognized no caste system. No one, and no group, could be singled out by the government for special spoliation.

The ability-to-pay doctrine proceeds from a direct viola-tion of this principle of equality.* It establishes a legal classification of society. It sets up a principle of government that was not contemplated when this nation was formed; it is a reversion to the caste system that had existed in Europe.

The easy argument that is used to slide this caste idea into our law is that those who are rich became so because they enjoy more of the benefits of government and therefore ought to pay more of its expenses. Is that so? Did the gov-

---

* Ability-to-pay is now taught as a sound basis of taxation in most college economics textbooks. One book that has achieved wide circulation is *Economics*, by John Ise. Typical of the line of reasoning which is fed to our youth is the following quotation from this book:

"Students of political science insist, however, that an economic oligarchy like the United States cannot be a political democracy in the best sense; that inevitably a few powerful capitalists and financiers will assume power in political affairs, which is inconsistent with genuine democracy; and the only way to maintain a real political democracy is to restore economic democracy through progressive taxation or otherwise." (Page 619.)

Despite such devious logic, the professor cannot avoid a gleam of sense. On the very next page of his textbook he says: "Any tax on man-made wealth or on income therefrom is a penalty on industry and thrift and an encouragement to laziness, improvidence and incompetence." Then he adds, "Yet it is inevitable that taxes should be levied in this way because the state must get revenues from people who have the money." So, our students are being taught that it is right to get where the getting is good.

29

ernment make them rich? If so, then the government is at fault; the only way the government can enrich a citizen is by giving him a special advantage over other citizens, and in that case the government violates its trust.

The government has nothing of its own to give, for it is not a producer of wealth. In granting one citizen a special advantage it automatically creates a disadvantage for other citizens. Thus, if it grants me tariff protection, it compels those who buy my merchandise to pay a higher price than they would have had to pay for similar merchandise from abroad; that extra price is my advantage, my customers' disadvantage. Or, if the government subsidizes my rent, it simply takes from other citizens what it hands me; it enriches me at the expense of other citizens.

It is obvious that in handing out special privileges the government is doing what it ought not to do; it is using its power not for the purpose of dispensing justice, but for the purpose of creating injustice. This is in violation of the principle of equality, and the violation is not corrected by taxing some of the proceeds of privilege; the privileges should be abolished. If I have acquired wealth by way of a special privilege granted me by the government, then when it lays a tax on my ill-gotten wealth it is sharing my unfair advantage; it is, so to say, a partner in my loot.

The advocates of ability-to-pay, however, do not distinguish between wealth obtained by production and wealth obtained by privilege. They simply assert that one could not get rich unless one operated under a government. This is true only in the sense that if there were no government to maintain order and protect property no one would try to acquire property; in a society where thievery is prevalent, production must fall to the point of mere subsistence. But the protection afforded to any one citizen is afforded to all; that is why men institute governments.

It is not police protection that makes one rich, the other poor. The differences in personal wealth that arise in any society—barring special privileges granted by government—are due either to accident or to qualities inherent in the individual: industry, thrift, abstinence. But it so happens that those who have and exercise these qualities do not injure others; their very substance indicates that in acquiring it they have benefited their fellowmen. If I become rich by making and selling shoes, it follows that many people have found my shoes desirable, and they have thus profited by my efforts. The wealth of society is in proportion to the productive efforts of the individuals who compose that society, and government has nothing to do with it—beyond the negative function of maintaining order and protecting property. *People make wealth; government can only take it.*

The effect of the ability-to-pay doctrine in practice is to discourage production. If an increasing portion of what I earn is taken from me—and that is the intent of the graduated income tax—then my inclination will be to cut down on my earnings. Men work to satisfy their desires, not to pay taxes. There is no sense in keeping my barn full if the highwayman empties it regularly and I have no means of preventing him from so doing. It is true that despite heavy income taxes men will try to keep up their standard of living by greater productive effort; but there comes a point where "what's the use?" impels them to adjust themselves to a lower standard of living. Why expand my business, why work overtime when my increased income will leave me

31

little for myself? It isn't worth it. That is the effect of the ability-to-pay doctrine.

If we examine the income tax carefully we find that it is not a tax on income so much as it is a tax on capital. What the government takes from me is not what I consume but what I might have saved. To be sure, I might have spent some of it for a new suit or to paint my house, but some of it I might have put in the bank, where it would have become available, at interest, to someone who would have used it to build a new factory, enlarge his plant, open a store, or buy a farm. That's what generally happens to savings. Certainly, a good part of the earnings of a corporation are put to plant improvement or expansion, which it cannot effect if the earnings are confiscated. *Hence, the effect of income taxation is to impair the capital structure of the country.*

Since all wages come out of production, and since the amount of production is in proportion to the amount of capital in use, it follows that the income tax, by depleting capital investment, tends to reduce both job opportunities and wages. Furthermore, the goods that are not produced because of the lack of capital surely do not help the consumer; the less goods on the market the higher the prices he must pay. *The income tax therefore hurts the wage earner to a far greater extent than by what is filched from his pay envelope.* It hurts him by increasing his cost of living and reducing his earning power.

Even the government must suffer, in the long run, from ability-to-pay taxation. Carried to its ultimate conclusion, this kind of levy must become so discouraging to the goose that lays the golden egg that it will stop laying, and the government that caused this condition will have no egg to live on. Of course, it can then try to use the capital it confiscated to produce goods, something to tax; it can go into business to replace the vacuum it created. That is socialism, which might be all right if it worked. It is not our province here to prove that state capitalism (socialism) is inefficient, that it produces very little besides deficits; witness, our Post Office Department. *When all the capital in the country is in the hands of the government, then all of us must work for the government under the conditions it prescribes—and that is slavery.* Which is the end product of ability-to-pay.

Despite all the long words and moral platitudes that have been used to shore up ability-to-pay, the fact is that this doctrine is closely related to the rule of highwaymanry: take where the taking is good. Those who practice that trade have the good grace not to moralize about it; they pick on the traveler who looks opulent and pass up the obvious bum. The government does likewise, and like the highwayman it does not quibble over how the victim came by his wealth.

The Sixteenth Amendment specifically says that the government may tax incomes "from whatever source derived." That means it may tax the earner, the gambler, the secondstory man, the highjacker, the housemaid, the prostitute. The highwayman is also undiscriminating, save as to ability to come across.*

* "In this country we neither create nor tolerate any distinction of rank, race or color, and should not tolerate anything else than entire equality in our taxes. So, then, I think the proposition [progressive income taxation] cannot be justified on any sound principle of morals. It can only be justified on the same ground that the highwayman defends his acts. It is saying to the man of wealth, 'you have got the money and we will take it because we can make better use of it than you will.'" Representative Morrill, May 23, 1866.

CHAPTER V

The Revolution of 1913

THE CIVIL WAR income-tax law, or laws, underwent several changes; but each change specified the same terminal date, 1870. Political promises being what they are, the last law was continued until 1872. This adherence to a terminal date is worth noting; it is a left-handed admission that the taxation of incomes was generally held to be obnoxious, perhaps unconstitutional, and was tolerated only as a temporary necessity. It was a war measure. Several Congressmen, from time to time, offered bills for the resumption of these taxes, but their efforts died a-borning. Two generations had to come and go, and two depressions had to be suffered, before Americans were ready to accept complacently the confiscation of their property. A quick look at the economic causes of this moral deterioration is in order.

The period after the Civil War was characterized by the customary boom followed by the inevitable bust. War stimulates productive activity, and the habit carries over into the peacetime. Everybody keeps on being busy. And everybody keeps on buying because everybody has a lot of the bogus money issued by the government during the war; also, everybody has bonds which can be cashed in or borrowed upon. The boom is on.

34

The post-Civil War boom was accelerated by the promise of the West; the prairie was being penetrated by miles and miles of railroad. It seemed that prosperity not only was here to stay, but that it would be a constantly expanding prosperity. Men gambled on it. They speculated on the future; they bought pieces of the future in the form of land and industrial securities, and paid prices that were based on the belief that people would grow richer and richer, forevermore.

In 1873 the inevitable depression set in. A depression is a halting of production. Production stops when people cut down on their consumption. They are compelled to curtail because they burdened themselves with obligations during the boom and now they are unable to meet the interest payments. Values did not rise as fast as they had expected; mortgages and other debts hang heavy on their necks, and in an effort to save their original investment they cut down on their consumption. Cutting down on consumption means putting people out of jobs, and so the whole house of cards collapses. Only when the false values are liquidated, the mortgages wiped out, can there be a resumption of production. The depression is a period of deflation following a period of inflation.

But hungry people are impatient. They cannot wait for deflation to wipe out the debris of their own orgy. A much quicker cure is called for, and the medicine that promises a quick cure is money. During the war, it was reasoned, the government printed greenbacks and there was prosperity; why not print more greenbacks and force prosperity to come back? And so, during the depression of 1873-76, and for twenty years after, there was a loud clamor for greenbacks, plus silver money to supplement the scarce gold.

35

This was the principal recipe of the social doctors of the times, a loud-mouthed lot who acquired the generic name of Populists.

These do-gooders were most vocal in the new West, where the "hard times" hit hardest and held on for the longest time. The story of this area is the story of the railroads. In the light of later experience, we can describe the railroad expansion of the 1880's as a make-work program, fostered by government subsidies and bounties. There was no economic need for most of these railroads. They were not built to serve an existing population, but to attract population from the eastern seaboard and from Europe. They amounted to a suburban land promotion. Even before they were built, when the companies had only pieces of paper giving them franchise rights, the bonanza that awaited prospective "empire builders" was advertised. All one needed to do to cash in on this promise was to buy a piece of land from the railroad companies, land which they had got for nothing from the government and which was still worthless and would continue to be worthless until settlers made them productive. With a gleam in their eyes, the settlers paid the companies' price by pledging their future earnings on the land; they mortgaged themselves to the hilt. Of course, their earnings would prove for a long time to be insufficient to meet their living expenses as well as the interest on the mortgages. Add to this sad picture the high freight rates which the monopolistic railroads charged them, and you have a panorama of gloom.

The plight of these farmers was made worse by the protective-tariff policy of the government. The best they could get for their products was the competitive world price, while the manufactures they bought, from the East, were loaded down with duties. Next to their demand for more money, the Populists clamored for lower tariffs.

It is not difficult to see that the boom and the bust were stimulated, if not caused, by acts of government, aided and abetted by the natural cupidity of people. But a people who feel a sense of hurt are not likely to look for basic causes, and are surely not inclined to blame themselves. They must have a "villain" on whom to vent their spleen; just as a child is satisfied when the mother spanks the wall against which the child has struck its head.

So, during the latter part of the nineteenth century, Americans took to the class-war doctrine recently imported by the socialists; here was a plausible cause of all their misfortunes, a logical scapegoat for their dissatisfaction. And the words that hung on the lips of the country were "plutocracy" and "robber barons" and "bloated rich" and "money bags," with suitable overtones. Also, since the opulence of the country was concentrated in the East, sectionalism added fire to the class-war doctrine, and "Wall Street" became the ultimate cause of all the economic ills of the country.°

The socialists had also imported the idea of a graduated income tax. Their prophet had written that this is the ideal instrument for destroying the hated capitalistic system, and they were in duty bound to promote it. It took Americans

---

° A typical remark in the debate on income taxation in the debate of 1894 is the following from the speech by Sen. Wm. A. Peffer, on June 21: "The only object we have in view in presenting this amendment [graduated income tax] is to rake in where there is something to rake in, not to throw out the dragnet where there is nothing to catch. The West and the South have made you people rich."

37

a long time to see eye-to-eye with the socialists on this matter of abolishing capitalism, for the tradition of private property was too strongly imbedded in their culture; but the income tax appealed to them as a means of wreaking their vengeance on those they hated—that is, those who had more than they had. By 1891, the Populists, who had by that time coagulated into the People's Party, included an income-tax plank in their platform; the Democratic Party later appropriated it.

Lots of learned treatises have been written on income taxation, and a wealth of erudition has been expended in its support. But when one looks to bottom causes one finds them quite simple:

Income taxation appeals to the governing class because in its everlasting urgency for power it needs money.

Income taxation appeals to the mass of people because it gives expression to their envy; it salves their sense of hurt.

The only beneficiaries of income taxation are the politicians, for it not only gives them the means by which they can increase their emoluments but it also enables them to improve their importance. The have-nots who support the politicians in the demand for income taxation do so only because they hate the haves; although they delude themselves with the thought that they might get some of the pelf, the fact is that the taxing of incomes cannot in any way improve their economic condition. *So that, the sum of all the arguments for income taxation comes to political ambition and the sin of covetousness.*

In 1893 the country had a new depression and a new president. Grover Cleveland, though endowed with more

38

integrity than the run-of-the-mill politician, nevertheless had to "do something" to satisfy the dissident elements. He asked Congress to lower tariffs and to make up this loss of government revenue with a tax on corporation incomes. Congress, heeding the screams of the Populists and the bombast of William Jennings Bryan, put through a bill calling for a two-percent tax on all incomes, with variations, and a deeper cut in tariffs than the president requested. This bill (which became law without Cleveland's signature) was declared unconstitutional by the Supreme Court before it became effective. The arguments for and against the bill, and some comments by the Court, are worth noting in the light of our later experience. But we might digress for a moment to examine the use of a demand for tariff reduction to introduce income taxation.

A tariff duty is a tax on consumption, and it is a tax from which the protected manufacturers derive a profit. The Populists, representing areas that had no manufactures, quite soundly denounced tariffs as an imposition on farmers and wage earners and as a special privilege conferred upon a small class in the East. The argument had too much weight to be easily ignored. Yet, the fact was that the government depended on tariffs for nearly half its revenue, and a cut in tariffs was a threat to the United States Treasury. For this argument the Populists were prepared with their cherished "soak the rich" proposal, the income tax. Hence, the bill of 1894 and the several income-tax bills introduced later, linked tariff reduction with income taxation. Not until the constitutional amendment was passed by Congress was the fiction dropped that tariff reduction and income taxation are related.

The Populists, as do all reformers, assumed that social good can be achieved through political action. They ignored the age-old fact that whenever the government does "good" it acts in the interests of some at the expense of others, meanwhile acquiring power for itself. *The end product of government intervention in the economy of the country is more power for government.* It never gives up power; it never abdicates.

Hence, the idea that the government would give up tariff revenue in exchange for income-tax revenue was contrary to all experience. It promised to make the swap, and perhaps its leaders believed the promise, but the nature of government is such that it cannot give up one power for another; not permanently, at any rate.

The historic fact is that tariffs rose higher than ever after income taxation was ultimately constitutionalized.° The income tax so enriched the Treasury that the revenue from tariffs became unimportant, and the government could afford to give more and more protection to the manufacturers; not only did the government thus gain the political support of the manufacturers, but it also shared in their tariff-enlarged profits through the income tax. If the government did not have the income tax it could not have raised the tariffs so high as to make importations impossible except for luxury goods. For, in order to get revenue the

---

° The Fordney-McCumber Tariff Act of 1922 (with an average ad valorem rate of 33 22 percent) restored the high protective tariff of pre-income-tax days. Ironically, the agricultural bloc of the Middle West and the South that had fought for the income tax, to enable a reduction in tariffs, joined with their erstwhile opponents to enact this bill. The highest tariff schedule in American history, with an average ad valorem rate of 40.08 percent, was passed in 1930. It was the Hawley-Smoot Tariff Act.

government would have had to encourage importations by keeping tariffs low. It would have had to pursue a tariff-for-revenue policy rather than a protective policy. The effect of income taxation on tariffs can be seen when we reflect that in 1894 the government's income from tariff duties amounted to 44 percent of its total revenues, while in 1950 less than 2 percent came from that source.

However, the Wilson tariff bill of 1894, with income-tax attachment, was passed. It was passed for two reasons: first, it reflected the growing "soak the rich" enthusiasm of Americans; second, it catered to the socialistic idea that was getting hold, namely, that the government is the ideal agency for the economic redemption of mankind. How much headway this second notion had made can be guessed when one reads the following argument by Representative David De Armond, of Missouri:

"The passage of the [Wilson] bill will mark the dawn of a brighter day, with more sunshine, more of the songs of birds, more of that sweetest music, the laughter of children, well fed, well clothed, well housed. Can we doubt that in the bright, happier days to come, good, even-handed Democracy shall be triumphant? God hasten the era of equality in taxation and in opportunity. And God prosper the Wilson bill, the first leaf in the book of reform in taxation, the promise of a brightening future for those whose genius and labor create the wealth of the land, and whose courage and patriotism are the only sure bulwark and defense of the Republic."

The do-gooding promises of such bilge, with which the debate was liberally sprinkled, were not implemented with

41

specific "social" legislation, the kind that came upon the country when income taxation attained fulfillment. But, they bespoke the secret desire for a golden calf to lead Americans to the promised land. They prepared the ground for Big Government.

It should be pointed out, however, that throughout the debate emphasis was placed on raising money only for the proper expense of government.* None of the advocates of income taxation spoke of expanding the functions of government, and while the opposition mentioned "socialism" it seems doubtful that they had any idea of a New Deal. The American mind of the nineteenth century was incapable of comprehending paternalism, regulation, and control; it was too strongly rooted in the past for that. Even those who advocated the tax method of undermining private property were not aware of what they were doing, and would probably have stopped in their tracks if they could have foreseen the consequences of their proposal. It was not any urgency for Big Government—which they could not even have understood—that prompted them to advocate income taxation. *It was simply an urgency to "soak the rich"—the very common sin of envy.*

The debate is heavily spiced with the desire to pare down fortunes, and for further relish there was a generous dash of sectionalism. For the fortunes that irritated their envy

* Even the staunchest advocates of income taxation, in those days, stressed only the need of revenue, though they suspected the possibility of the taxation-for-social-purposes doctrine that followed the adoption of the Sixteenth Amendment. Thus, Sen. Williams, on August 26, 1913: "We do not want to collect any more revenue than we need. . . . Having concluded that we had enough, we are not taxing people's income even for fun, nor are we taxing them for the purpose of building up a system."

were located in the East; they were after "foreigners," not neighbors. For example, Senator William A. Peffer, of Kansas, who, by the way, was even more "advanced" than the bill in that he advocated a graduated income tax, expostulated thus:

"The point to be made is that because wealth is accumulated in New York, and not because those men are more industrious than we are, not because they are wiser or better, but because they trade, because they buy and sell, because they deal in usury, because they reap in what they never earned, because they take in and live off what other men earn, they shall be exempt from taxation, and that we who are hewing wood and carrying water shall continue to bear the burdens of government."

William Jennings Bryan, of Nebraska, spoke for the impoverished West when he said:

"Gentlemen have denounced the income tax as class legislation because it will affect more people in one section of the country than in another. Because the wealth of the country is, to a large extent, centered in certain cities and states does not make a bill sectional which imposes a tax in proportion to wealth. If New York and Massachusetts pay more tax under this law than other states, it will be because they have more taxable incomes within their borders. And why should not those sections pay most which enjoy most?"

In reading these speeches one wonders whether there ever would have been an income tax in this country if the advocates of it could have held off until Chicago was able to

43

stand up to New York, and Nebraska farmers, sporting limousines, became the envy of Boston workers. Even the opponents of the bill seemed little aware of the concentration of political power that income taxation would generate, and directed their arguments mostly to the principle of private property, to the unconstitutionality of the bill, to the doctrine of class legislation. Bourke Cockran, Representative from New York, almost touched on the vital subject when he said:

> "... to persuade a majority to oppress a minority is not to serve the people but to injure them; it is not to vindicate popular power, but to discredit it; it is not to conserve free institutions, but to undermine republican government."

After the bill was passed, and it came to the Supreme Court, some references to the subject of individual rights and limited government were made; there seemed to be no awareness that income taxation might destroy the American tradition of freedom.* Thus, Justice Field, in a brilliant argument supporting the majority opinion declaring the bill unconstitutional, quotes approvingly the point brought up by counsel:

> "There is no such thing in the theory of our national government as unlimited power of taxation in Congress. There are limits of its powers arising out of the essential nature of all free governments; there are reservations of individual

---

* It was not until 1937 that the Supreme Court, through the mouth of Justice Benjamin Cardozo, had the forthrightness to declare that "natural rights, so-called, are as much a subject of taxation as rights of lesser importance."

44

rights, without which society could not exist, and which are respected by every government. The right of taxation is subject to these limitations."

The seed of class hatred that had been planted during the Civil War proved fertile. Its sprout was merely stunted by the 1895 decision of the Supreme Court. In the years following, it continued to send forth shoots that circumvented the Constitution, for under the guise of "excise" taxation, levies were laid on some corporation incomes and on inheritances. The Spanish-American War created a climate favorable to these taxes, and the Supreme Court, in 1900, did some major logic-chopping to justify the legislation; in fact, the decision of 1900, which was a piece of legislation in itself, was of great help later to those who wanted general income taxation.

The drumfire of "soak the rich" was having its effect. Even the rich began to join in the chorus. The wealthy are of course no more motivated by principle than the poor; expediency and convenience shape the thoughts and guide the behavior of the millionaire as well as the worker's. Even as "Park Avenue," in our times, mouths communistic phrases in order to appear "advanced," so in the early part of the century some of the wealthy assumed a "democratic" pose and spoke nice words about income taxation.° Professors of economics would not be left behind; the "progressive" thing to do was to write erudite articles in support of ability-to-pay. The mob had captured the intelligentsia, even as it

° "I know that some of the wealthiest men in this country support it [income taxation]. I know that Mr. Gould in an interview favored it, and I am told by the gentleman from Missouri that Mr. Carnegie favors it." Rep. Bourke Cockran, Jan. 30, 1894.

led the politicians; the aristocratic champion of the masses, Theodore Roosevelt, advocated progressive inheritance taxation in 1906, and in his 1908 message to Congress he urged an income tax.

When William Howard Taft became president, not only the Democrats but also an "insurgent" segment of the Republicans had been captured by the Populist philosophy, and the combination worked strenuously to put over the "great reform." As usual, an income-tax amendment to a tariff bill was proposed. Mr. Taft, a former judge, opposed this amendment because he was solicitous for the reputation of the Supreme Court, which would be compromised whether it upheld or reversed the decision of 1895. A political deal was put over; the tariff bill was passed with a rider taxing corporation incomes, and the opposition was promised a bill for a constitutional amendment. This promise was later kept by the Republican leadership, which was opposed to income taxation; they were sure that not enough states would ratify the bill. By 1913, forty-two states did ratify it, and the Sixteenth Amendment became part of the Constitution.

In name, it was a tax reform. In point of fact, it was a revolution.

For the Sixteenth Amendment corroded the American concept of natural rights; ultimately reduced the American citizen to a status of subject, so much so that he is not aware of it; enhanced Executive power to the point of reducing Congress to innocuity; and enabled the central government to bribe the states, once independent units, into subservience. No kingship in the history of the world ever exercised more power than our Presidency, or had more of the people's wealth at its disposal. We have retained the forms and phrases of a republic, but in reality we are living under an oligarchy, not of courtesans, but of bureaucrats.

It had to come to that. The theory of republican government is that sovereignty resides in the citizen, who lends it to his elected representative for a specified time. But a people whose wealth is siphoned into the coffers of its government is in no position to stand up to it; with its wealth goes its sovereignty, its sense of dignity. People still vote, of course, but their judgment in the ballot booth is unduly influenced by handouts from their government, whether these be in the form of "relief," parity prices, or orders for battleships. Though it is not exactly an over-the-counter transaction, the citizen's conscience is bought. Nor are voters immune to the propaganda issued by the bureaucrats, in their own behalf, and paid for by the voters themselves.

With America's immunity of property went the immunity of body. Notice that Mr. Lincoln had great difficulty in enforcing a moderate form of conscription, even in wartime; now we have peacetime conscription, apparently as a permanent policy. Mr. Lincoln had difficulty with his draft because he did not have the wherewithal to hire an army of enforcement agents. Thanks to the income tax, our present government is not so handicapped. Resistance is so dangerous that we have made a virtue of compliance; the conscript army is described as a "democratic" army, and the conscientious objector is often looked down upon as little better than a traitor. So completely have we become adjusted to this detestable practice of the Czars, that every mother is recon-

47

ciled to the fact that her newborn son will be a soldier if, unfortunately, he grows up sound of mind and body.

While we are on this subject of immunity of the body, we should mention the fact that though we long ago abolished debtors' prisons, we do have prisons for those who violate the income-tax laws. We can cheat one another with impunity, but not the government. So thorough and so ruthless is the machinery of tax collections that it is used to catch and incarcerate suspected criminals against whom legal evidence of criminality cannot be adduced. Professional gamblers, hoodlums, and racketeers of all sorts, aware of the swift and certain punishment dealt out by the minions of the income-tax law, are scrupulous in the making out of their tax reports. Thus, the Sixteenth Amendment, enacted to increase the government's revenues, has spawned another police department, another means of forcing the citizen into line.

The third great immunity is that of the mind, the freedom to think as one wishes. The impairment of this immunity is not easy to detect, for the operation can be conducted in such a way that the victim is never aware of it. It is necessary to look at the methods employed by the government to shape thought, to know that the shaping is being done; when the job is completed it takes a keen observer to realize that people think differently from the way they used to think.

Thus, the farmer who receives checks for not planting does not realize that his grandfather would have thought the practice immoral; he accepts the taking of gratuities as the regular order of things, as quite proper, because government propaganda has got him into that frame of mind. Free school lunches do not strike the modern mother as an insult,

48

as suggesting that she is unable and unwilling to carry out the responsibility of motherhood; the convenience of free lunches, plus the saving of expense, plus the government's leaflets have changed her way of thinking. And so with every activity of government turned Santa Claus by the income tax: *a mass of propaganda introduces the new practice and more propaganda justifies it, until the people think as the government wants them to think.* Free judgment becomes next to impossible.

Not content with direct propaganda, the opulent government goes in for shaping the mind of the future by invading the educational machinery. In this it is aided by the very operation of the income tax. The rich cannot be as generous with their contributions to the colleges as they used to be, for the government has the money that they might have given. So the government comes to the rescue of these institutions with grants. It cannot be said with certainty that the government determines the curricula of the colleges as a condition of the grants. But the generosity cannot fail to impress the professors, particularly since the professors have learned to look forward to jobs in the ever-growing bureaucracy.

It is interesting to note that in nearly all the economics courses it is taught that the income tax is the proper instrument for the regulation of the country's economy; that private property is not an inalienable right (in fact, there are no inalienable rights); that the economic ills of the country are traceable to the remnants of free enterprise; that the economy of the nation can be sound only when the government manages prices, controls wages, and regulates operations. This was not taught in the colleges before 1913.

49

Is there a relationship between the results of the income tax and the thinking of the professors?

There is now a strong movement in this country to bring the public-school system under federal domination. The movement could not have been thought of before the government had the means for carrying out the idea; that is, before income taxation. The question is, have those who plug for nationalization of the schools come to the idea by independent thought, or have they been influenced by the bureaucrats who see in nationalization a wider opportunity for themselves? We must lean to the latter conclusion, because among the leaders of the movement are many bureaucrats. However, if the movement is successful, if the schools are brought under the watching eye of the federal government, it is a certainty that the curriculum will conform to the ideals of Big Government. The child's mind will never be exposed to the idea that the individual is the one big thing in the world, that he has rights which come from a higher source than the bureaucracy.

Thus, the immunities of property, body and mind have been undermined by the Sixteenth Amendment. The freedoms won by Americans in 1776 were lost in the revolution of 1913.

CHAPTER VI

Soak the Poor

"FROM ANY source derived" includes wages. To be sure, the original Populists, and the aping Democrats and Republicans, to say nothing of the conscious Socialists, little thought that their income-tax gadget would ever be used to "soak the poor." It was an instrument, they thought, that could lend itself to no other purpose than to expropriate the rich in favor of the poor. How the poor would benefit from the expropriation, they did not explain; their intense hatred of the rich conveniently filled this vacuum in their argument. Their passion blinded them to the fact that this "soak the rich" law would enable the government to filch the pay envelope.

The class-war doctrine is most vicious not in that it sets man against man, producer against producer, but in that it diverts the attention of the contestants from their common enemy, the State. *Men live by production, but the State lives by appropriation.* While the haves and the have-nots struggle over the division of existing wealth, it is the business of the State to improve itself at the expense of both; it picks up the marbles while the boys are fighting. That has been the story of men in organized society since the beginning. That this lesson of history should have escaped the reformers of the nineteenth century, when the habit of freedom was still strong in America, can be easily understood; what is not easily explained is the acceptance of the doctrine of benevolent government in our day, when all the evidence to the contrary is before our eyes.

However, one good "reason" followed another for making better use of the Sixteenth Amendment. After 1913, the government, which for over a century had managed to get along without income taxation, felt a continuing need for more funds.* The income-tax rates kept climbing, and the exemptions kept declining; the mesh of the dragnet was made finer and finer so that more fish could be caught. At first it was the incomes of corporations, then of rich citizens, then of well-provided widows and opulent workers, and finally the wealth of housemaids and the tips of waitresses.

This is all in line with the ability-to-pay doctrine. *The poor, simply because there are more of them, have more ability to pay than the rich.* The national pay envelope contains more money than the combined treasuries of all the corporations of the country. The government could not for long overlook this rich mine. Political considerations, however, made the tapping of the pay envelope difficult. The wage earners have votes, many votes, and in order not to alienate these votes, it was necessary to devise some means for making the taxation of their incomes palatable. They had to be lulled into acceptance of "soak the poor."

The drug that was concocted for this purpose was "social

* For a number of years between 1801 and 1890, except during the Civil War, the revenues of the country equaled its expenses or sometimes showed an embarrassing surplus.

security." The worker was told that he was not paying an income tax when his pay envelope was opened and robbed; he was simply making a "contribution" to "insurance" against the inevitable disabilities of old age. He would get it all back, when he could no longer work, and with a profit.

This is sheer fraud, as can be readily seen when comparison between social security and legitimate insurance is made. When you pay a premium on an insurance policy, the company keeps part of it in reserve. The amount thus set aside is based on actuarial experience; the company knows from long study how much money it must keep on hand to meet probable claims. Most of your premium is invested in productive business, and out of the earnings from such investment the company pays its running expenses and builds up a surplus to meet unexpected strains; or it pays the policy holders a share of this extra income, in dividends. Without going into the intricate details of the insurance business, the guiding principle is that benefits are paid out of the reserve or the company's earnings from investments.

Is that what happens to your "contribution" to social security? Not a bit of it.

Every cent taken from wages is thrown into the till of the United States Treasury, and is spent for anything the government decides upon. So, too, are the "contributions" from the employer. That is to say, social-security taxes are taxes, pure and simple; they are "forced dues and charges" levied by the sovereign on his subjects for the expenses of state. None of the money is held in reserve, none of it is invested in business. All is spent, and it is spent long before the "insured" is entitled to benefits.

53

To give some plausibility to the "insurance" advertisement, the government sets up a so-called reserve fund. In place of the money it collects, it piles up its own bonds, or I.O.U.'s, in an amount equal to the collections. The interest on these bonds, it says, will be adequate to meet the old-age obligations when due. But the interest on these bonds is paid out of what it collects in taxes; where else can the government get money? Since the so-called premiums are only taxes, and since the benefit payments are also taxes, the operation is the same as if an insurance company used up its premium collections in salaries and cocktail parties and then paid out benefits from new premiums. For doing that, the directors of the company can be sent to jail. However, the laws made for ordinary citizens are somewhat different from the laws made for public officials.

One of the arguments which helped to sell social security is that the "contributor" will not be dependent on his children for a livelihood when he can no longer work. Let's see if that is true. We must keep in mind that taxes are part of production; they are levied on what is being produced currently, not in the past. The payments to the nonproductive aged therefore come from what the government collects from those who are producing, their children. The government cannot get the money from anybody else. *So that, in effect, the children are supporting their parents, collectively and without love.*

The swindle is further compounded by the promise of something-for-nothing. The worker is told that his employer, the "exploiter," pays part of the premium, and is in effect compelled to make a contribution to old-age benefits. The fact is, as every schoolboy should know, that *the employer must include in his expenses what he is compelled to "contribute." This expense shows up in the price of his goods, and the wage earner, as consumer, actually pays it.* There is a similarity in this scheme with the shell game at the county fair.

The more we look into this offspring of the Sixteenth Amendment the more we are astounded by its fraudulent character. Take the matter of the bonds in the reserve fund. The government can issue money against them—that is, it can "buy" them with printed money when it needs money to pay old-age benefits; that is part of the law. Or, if the government sells the bonds to private persons, or to the banks, the buyers can borrow against them. In either case, new money comes into the market, lowering the volume of all the money in existence. That is inflation. Now, *the money taken from the worker's pay envelope is worth more, will buy more goods, than the money he will get when he is old, simply because these bonds are in existence.* This social-security scheme was started in 1937. One does not have to be an economist to know that in 1937 the dollar bought more bread and shoes than it does in 1954. The man who in 1954 begins drawing old-age benefits gets dollars that will fetch him less of the things he needs than the dollars he was compelled to "contribute" in 1937 and during the years that followed.

When the law was put into effect, the social-security doctors figured out that the fund will have to reach fifty billions of dollars before the interest on the bonds will be enough to pay the stipulated benefits to all who are entitled to it. That is, if the stipulated benefits are not increased. However, for political reasons there have been changes in

55

both the benefits and the number of people who have been forced into the scheme. The "premiums" have also been raised. These changes have been made under the name of "insurance," but the plain fact is that the government made them in order to increase its spendable funds. *It wanted more taxes, and it dipped further into the pay envelope; that is the real purpose of the social-security laws.**

At this writing, the fictitious reserve fund has accumulated fifteen billions in bonds. Already some economists are beginning to wonder how the government will be able to pay benefits to all those who during the past sixteen years have been making "contributions" when they will have reached the age of sixty-five. Figurers have shown that the interest will not be sufficient to keep the aged barely alive, if they have to depend on these stipends; and under the law they are deprived of these stipends if they earn more than $75 a month extra. This is the answer:

The government will meet its obligations by handing out brand-new printed dollars, with declining purchasing power, and the old folks will have to depend on what support they can beg from their tax-ridden children.

This book deals with income taxation, not with social security, which needs a book in itself. But we started out

---

* Initially, the "social security" tax was 1 percent of all taxable wages up to $3,000 per annum, paid by both employer and employee. In 1951, the tax was extended to wages of $3,600. In 1951, also, "self-employed" persons were pulled in; now they too must pay for "social security," whether they want the "insurance" or not, and the rate, which was set at 2¼ percent in 1951, rises each year until it reaches the maximum of 4¾ percent in 1970. The rates on employer and employee also rise from the initial rate of 1 percent to the 1970 limit of 3¼ percent.

with the purpose of showing how the Sixteenth Amendment changed our country economically, politically, and morally, and there is no better example of this change than the operation of the social-security branch of income taxation and its effects on the character of the nation.

Despite the fact that social security is a fraud in every respect, there are many who, ignoring the evidence, support it because "we must not let the old folks suffer destitution." This implies that before 1937 it was habitual for children to cast their nonproductive parents into the gutter. There is no evidence for that, and there are no records supporting the implication that all over sixty-five regularly died of hunger. The present crop of children are just as considerate of their old folks as were the pre-1937 vintage, and it is a certainty that if their envelopes were not tapped they would be in better position to show their filial devotion. Besides, if the government did not take so much of our earnings, we would be better able to save for our later days.

The fact is, there is no such thing as *social* security; only the *individual* grows old and is in need. Society is never in want and never grows old, simply because society is not a person. Security against the exigencies of old age has always been a problem of life, and each person in his own way has tried to solve it. Paying up the mortgage on the old home so that one would always have a roof over one's head was one way; laying up a nest egg was another; annuity insurance is the most recent form of security.

These methods of taking care of oneself through thrift, however, call for self-reliance, and that is exactly what the advocates of social security would destroy. It is contrary to the whole philosophy of socialism. If the individual is

57

allowed to shift for himself, there is no need for the services of the self-anointed do-gooders. Hence it is necessary to develop a slave psychology, a feeling of helpless dependence on the group. If this calls for the use of police power—and it always does—so much the better; that means the organization of a bureaucracy with a vested interest in continuing poverty.

Lurking in the background of social-security thinking is a concept of organized society that is gall and wormwood to fundamental Americanism. It is the idea that in the nature of things some men are destined to rule and others to obey. As a matter of fact, social-security advocates must take resort in the caste system of society to support their "insurance" scheme. They maintain that social security is necessary because most wage earners are incontinent and must be secured against their own weakness. Who is best qualified to look after them? Why, those who have been anointed with the proper college degrees and are crowned with the power of the State.

It was exactly this father-child concept of society that Bismarck held, and for that very reason he took to social security. In his political philosophy it was axiomatic that the Junker class was ordained by God to rule over Germany. As a correlative, it was an obligation of that class to look after the welfare of the ruled.°

In a feudal society, where the economy is almost wholly agricultural and people do not move from place to place, it

---

° Said Bismarck: "I acknowledge unconditionally a right to work and I will stand for it as long as I am in this place. But here I do not stand upon the ground of Socialism ... but on that of Prussian common law." Prussian common law, drawn up during several reigns, and finally codified and promulgated by Frederick II, contained the following:

was quite simple for the ruling lord to see that his sick and old tenants were provided for. But this direct relationship between ruler and ruled could not be maintained in an industrial economy, and in Bismarck's time, industry was upsetting the comfortable feudal system. Social security came to his rescue; it was just what he needed to make his feudal concept of government work.

If anybody could make social security work, it would have been the Junkers. They were by tradition and economic independence free from the petty temptations of office; they were not beholden to an electorate for either their income or their position. And yet, they were unable to build a healthy society upon social security.

The reason for the failure of social security in Germany, and wherever else it has been tried, is psychological, not political. *When the individual is relieved of the obligation of self-respect, he acquires the habits of helplessness; he is inclined to retreat to the security of the prenatal state. The more he is taken care of the more he wants care.*

In the past twenty years, thanks to the prevailing social-security philosophy, it has become a habit of mind with American youth to look upon government as its permanent guardian; the idea that one is responsible for onself is sneered at as "reaction." It is nearly impossible to convince a young man born after 1920 that to accept a government handout is degrading—or that the whole social-security business is a fraud.

---

1. It is the duty of the State to provide sustenance and support of its citizens who cannot . . . provide subsistence for themselves.

2. Work adapted to their strength and capacities shall be supplied. . . .

6. The State is entitled and is bound to take such measures as will prevent destitution of its citizens and check excessive extravagance.

There are some advocates of social security who maintain that it can be divorced from politics and run on sound insurance principles. It can, but not by the government; that, however, is not what is meant. It is assumed that the government can run an honest insurance business, sticking very close to actuarial figures in determining its policy payments. But how can a government business be rid of politics? Especially a government which rests on popular suffrage?

Any attempt to limit security payments by actuarial figures would raise a howl of protest, a howl that would be recorded at the next election. The politicians have convinced the American citizen that the government owes him a living, as a matter of "right," and what is easier than to ask for more? And the aspirant for office would have to be much above the average if he did not promise more. Were he to tell the citizen that the whole thing is a fraud, that only a private insurance company could manage the business on a sound basis, he would be inviting defeat at the polls.

In Germany, the social-security philosophy of government led to that moral decadence which facilitated the advent of Hitler. In England, it made a once-proud people into a nation of panhandlers. What will it do to America?

In 1943, taking advantage of the war, the federal government put further pressure on those of modest incomes; it enacted a law requiring employers to deduct twenty percent from the earner's pay envelope, or check, for the government's account. The government was spending money so fast that it could not wait until the end of the year for collections. It had to have its cut of income even before the earner saw it. In line with this urgency, it required corporations and business and professional men to pay every quarter, in advance, an estimated amount of their earnings.

Measures instituted by government during war have a way of perpetuating themselves during peacetime. Government is incapable of relinquishing powers. And so, the withholding and the pay-as-you-go taxes are still in force and will continue. And, of course, government will find good reason for spending money as fast as it comes in, or faster. Despite its monstrous take from production, and its means for expediting collections, its expenses exceed income, and the excess is annually taken care of by what is known as "deficit financing." This, as every spendthrift knows, is borrowing against expected income; it is borrowing against the future. *But while the private spendthrift is held in leash by the threat of bankruptcy, government is unhampered by any such fear; it can print money or something equivalent to money, and compel citizens and banks to accept this paper in payment for its debts; it can rob its subjects by the trick of inflation, and thus make up its overspending.*

The real reason for withholding taxes is the unwillingness of workers to share their incomes with the government and the consequent difficulties of collection. To overcome this handicap, the government has simply impressed employers into its service as involuntary and unpaid tax collectors. It is a form of conscription. Disregarding the right of privacy, which is an essential of liberty, the government's agents may, under the law, invade the employer's office, demand his accounts, and punish him for any infraction which they believe he has committed; they can impound his property and inflict a penalty for not having collected taxes for the government.

This violation of our vaunted rights was highlighted by Miss Vivien Kellems, a Connecticut manufacturer, several years ago. To test the constitutionality of the law, Miss Kellems refused to collect these taxes and notified the government of her intention. She asked that she be indicted so that the matter could be brought to court. At the same time, she instructed her employees to pay their taxes regularly, helped them compute the amounts, and saw to it that they had proof of payment. The government refused to indict her. Rather, its agents, without court order (the government is not hampered by such formalities), impounded her bank account and demanded a penalty from her for not collecting taxes which had been paid. The only thing she could do under the circumstances was to sue the government for recovery of her money. In this she was successful. But the matter of constitutionality was assiduously avoided by the government's attorneys, by legal tricks, and she was never able to get to it. Laws are made for citizens, not the government, to obey.

There is grave question as to the constitutionality of the withholding taxes. But that is not a point of consequence; the Constitution has often proved itself amenable to political considerations. *The main point is that the Sixteenth Amendment has widened the area of government power, and as a consequence has reduced the area of liberty.*

62

CHAPTER VII

Corruption and Corruption

*"The imposition of the [income] tax will corrupt the peo-
ple. It will bring in its train the spy and the informer. It will
necessitate a swarm of officials with inquisitorial powers. It
will be a step toward centralization. . . . It breaks another
canon of taxation in that it is expensive in its collection and
cannot be fairly imposed; . . . and, finally, it is contrary to
the traditions and principles of republican government."*—
REPRESENTATIVE ROBERT ADAMS, January 26, 1894.

THE WORD "corruption," in American usage, suggests
the use of office for the betterment of the politician. The
word has other meanings. The fact that this political meaning comes to mind first, indicates that the practice is
common. Is it because the men we put in office are of
particularly low character, innately, that political corruption
is so common, or is it because the opportunities to better
one's circumstances are so inviting in public office? Since
in our form of government the officials are not born into
it, but are drawn from private life, we must conclude that
they are no worse and no better than the rest of us, and
that their moral deterioration results from the temptations
political power generates. Therefore, the more political
power the more corruption. And political power concerned

directly with the nation's wealth contains the most corruptive possibilities.

That corruption in the Internal Revenue Bureau runs high needs no proof. It would be easy to fill up many pages with "sensational" stuff by merely recounting what has appeared in the public press, even in the last few years. But that would be like serving up a full course of filth, disgusting and hardly illuminating. It is now part of American folklore that agents of the Internal Revenue Bureau have been amenable to bribery, that "pull" has played a part in the adjustment of disputed tax returns, that cases against tax dodgers have been quashed by higher-ups after field agents have conscientiously worked them up. The Bureau itself has made some disclosures of such malpractice, and the opposition party, always mindful of a "corruption" issue for the coming election, has made much of what it could dig up.

It would be miraculous if things were otherwise. The Internal Revenue Bureau is charged with the task of enforcing an immoral law, a law that violates the principle of private property. The taxpayer, even though he prates about his willingness to pay his "just share" of government expenses, always finds his "just share" unjust. And so it is. Even the doctrinaire socialist, while decrying the iniquity of private property, resents being deprived of his own; after all, the socialist is a human. *It is written into our consciousness that "mine is mine," and all the tomes in support of income taxation cannot wipe out that thought.*

The Internal Revenue Bureau quite sensibly takes the view that every one of us is a potential lawbreaker, as far as the income-tax law is concerned. To approach its task

64

with any other point of view would undermine its effectiveness. It has a war against society on its hands, and to win that war it must make use of the artifices of war, such as espionage, deception, and force. Society, on the other hand, though necessarily on the defensive, is not entirely helpless. It knows that the weakness of the Internal Revenue Bureau is the fact that its operatives are also human. They too are always on the lookout for an easy dollar. Thus, the natural inclination of the agent blends with the natural inclination of the taxpayer to form a setting for the circumvention of the unnatural law. Why expect anything else? If this setting produces corruption, we must look to the law, not to the human beings involved, for cause.

Aiding the agent in his collusion with the taxpayer is the disparity of numbers in this struggle; the potential lawbreakers are entirely too numerous for the handful of collectors. If the number of enforcement agents were to be increased to a proper balance, the cost would eat into the "profits" of the operation. For political reasons, it is necessary for the IRB to show that the cost of collection is little, compared to the amount collected. Knowing this, and knowing also that his usefulness to the Bureau is measured by the amount of the collections he is able to effect, the agent is inclined to settle a disputed tax case; if, incidentally, the settlement is topped with a clandestine gratuity, so much the better. One senator is currently making a name for himself by bringing to light settlements amounting to as little as a few cents on the dollar, when the taxpayer, although admitting his indebtedness to the government, proves he is virtually bankrupt. The Bureau's answer is that "something is better than nothing," and the senator, unable

65

to prove what he obviously suspects, must accept that sensible answer.

It is a certainty that the wage earner cannot be a party to such corruption; not that he is above it, but that he lacks opportunity; what is taken from his envelope is beyond settlement. Besides, what can he offer in the way of a bribe? Only the taxpayer in the higher brackets is in position to "do business" with officials. The "business" is aided by the complexities in the laws designed to tap their incomes. And these complexities, which result in interpretations, which encourage corruption, are unavoidable.

All taxes come from production. A tax law that stops production is self-defeating. Hence, in framing the statute the government must try to get all that the traffic will bear without stopping the traffic. The producer must be allowed to keep enough of his returns so that he will be able to continue to operate; the victim must not be strangulated. This presents a difficult problem in lawmaking, especially when the victim is a large and complicated business; or when the law seeks to cover every contingency in all the industries that make up the complicated national economy. The lawmakers must overlook something; they cannot anticipate every new scheme that man, in his desire to get along in the world, will think up. Therefore, "loopholes" in the law show up, and sometimes these loopholes are deliberately put into the law at the behest of some important pressure group.°

° A deliberate and most lucrative "loophole" is the exemption enjoyed by educational and religious organizations. It is common practice for these organizations to buy real estate and then rent the properties to the seller. The seller gets a long-term, low-rent lease, which the buyer is able to give because the income to a "nonprofit" institution is tax exempt. The American

The ingenious entrepreneur, trying to "beat the rap," will take advantage of the clauses in the law which were intended only to permit him to stay in business, after taxes. With the help of expert accountants, he finds ways of squeezing an extra dollar through the "loopholes," or discovers a "loophole" not intended by the lawmakers. But here he may come into conflict with the government's agent, whose opinion on what are legitimate expenses of business may differ from his. Was too much deducted for depreciation? Was the inventory taken at true value, and what is true value? How about those large expense accounts, that costly public-relations program? Are they necessary to the conduct of the business? The agent says this, the taxpayer says that, and thus we have the makings of a costly lawsuit. The natural inclination of the taxpayer is to seek some other way out, and sometimes the agent is quite amenable to "reason." *The corruption is written into the law.*

However, if corruption were limited to the mere giving or taking of bribes, direct and indirect, we could write it off as of secondary importance; it is simply the inevitable consequence incident to the operation of an immoral law. Of far greater concern is the use of income taxation to undermine the principles of republican government and to make a mockery of our tradition of freedom.

In 1931—that was before the arrogance of federal power had reached the point to which the administration of

Council of Education recently estimated that 40 percent of all university and college endowments are now invested in private enterprises, the earnings of which are nontaxable because they are put to educational use. The earnings of businesses operated by labor unions are also free of taxes, as are the earnings from the extensive real estate operations of the churches. Thus, a powerful vested interest in exemptions has grown up.

67

Franklin D. Roosevelt ultimately brought it—the infamous case of William H. Malone began. This man, who ran for Governor of Illinois on the Republican ticket in 1932, had been Chairman of the Illinois Tax Commission. In that position he had offended the Pullman Company and the Chicago Traction Lines; that is, he had made decisions unfavorable to the tax claims of these companies. Their resentment flowered into the passion of revenge. Somehow, the passion found expression in a case against Malone, instituted by the Internal Revenue Bureau, for "willful evasion" of his income taxes.

The case lasted six years. The record of the case, written up in a book entitled *They Got Their Man*, by Elmer Lynn Williams, indicates that witnesses were coerced and threatened, that bribes were tendered to secure an indictment, that the District Attorney, who later rose to a judgeship, conducted the trial with "the fury of a political feud." The presiding judge, who sentenced Malone to two years in the penitentiary, was known to be active in the campaign of the District Attorney for U. S. Senator. It should be pointed out that Malone had protested certain taxes levied against him, that he promised to pay the sum in dispute if the Board of Tax Appeals decided against him, that he cooperated with the investigating agents, as they themselves testified. Nevertheless, the charge was "willful evasion," which is a criminal offense, and Malone was sent to jail. He was a political undesirable.

Sixteen years later, a similar case sprang up in Boston. A sixty-four-year-old businessman decided to give his time and talents to public service. He ran on the Republican ticket for the General Council and was elected. Before his

68

election he had had some disagreement with the Labor Commissioner, who came from his own town. After election he recommended to the Governor the dismissal of this man from office. The ousted Labor Commissioner thirsted for revenge. He was a loyal member of the party in the federal saddle. Whether this had anything to do with it or not, the fact is that shortly after he had taken office, Alfred Calvin Gaunt was charged by the Internal Revenue Bureau with "willful evasion."

The case involved the matter of evaluating depreciation; there was a dispute over the value Gaunt put upon the plant in 1931, which in turn had a bearing on his tax returns. In the investigation, Gaunt, like Malone before him, hid nothing from the agents, but went out of his way to furnish them with every scrap of evidence in his possession as far back as they wanted to go. There was certainly nothing that could be called "moral turpitude" in his behavior or in his background, and it seemed that the most the Bureau could ask for would be additional taxes, based on a different evaluation of the plant, plus interest and penalties. The conduct of the case, however, indicates that the Bureau was acting under political pressure. They wanted Gaunt, not his money. They got him. He was sentenced to serve eighteen months in jail.

The two cases are identical in significance, and are here offered as examples because they occurred under different Washington administrations. The composition of the ruling regime makes no difference; the Internal Revenue Bureau is a self-operating inquisitorial body. *It has the means of harassing, intimidating, and crushing the citizen who falls into its disfavor.* In the two cases cited the starting point was a difference of opinion on the correctness of a bookkeeping entry. The Bureau could have sued for the recovery of taxes, a civil case; it chose to bring the criminal charge of "willful evasion." The Bureau has that choice. The tax laws are so intricate, and made more so by Bureau rulings and Tax Court decisions, that it is virtually impossible for an accountant to be sure his method of arriving at a taxable income, or his computation of the tax, is beyond question. The technicalities that the Bureau may bring up are legion. Therefore, whenever the Bureau has reason to "get" somebody it has ample means at its disposal. And its viciousness in pursuing a chosen victim, as in the cases mentioned, is unrelenting, simply because its reputation for success is at stake. It must not fail.

This is what the late Senator Schall of Minnesota had to say about this phase of corruption:

"The one glaring governmental agency that constitutes a menace to the citizens is the Income Tax Bureau, which often goes outside the constitutional limitations and frequently harasses citizens by unjust exactions and by the oppressive conduct of its agents. This system has one defect that is fundamental. That is its lack of certainty, involving not only the time and manner of payment but also the clear, definite and fixed amount. While the Bureau is a Babel of conflicting regulations and opinions, it believes it is so entrenched by authority granted and assumed, and by its anonymous character, that it even dares to attack the citizens by a charge of fraud without substantial pretext or cause. . . .

"The bureau is inquisitorial. It is bureaucracy. Washington is cluttered up with its offices. Its forces swarm over the country, and the cardinal doctrine under which it operates is to inspire the citizen with fear. Agents, spies and snoopers annoy and plague the citizens. The agents, rarely of high order in point of skill or character, must show some kind of results. The Bureau grades them for promotion to increased salary, or better still for the honor roll, not on what taxes are finally returned to the government, but by the amounts they mark up first or charge against the taxpayer.

"That practice permits and promotes, if it does not direct, a species of blackmail against the American citizen.... Once having started in pursuit, the agent assumes authority to impute fraud to the most innocent transactions, and the perfectly honest taxpayer must submit to indignities, odium and accusations of criminality and be put to heavy expense to prove to his own government that he is not a criminal."

Nor is that all. There have been cases—for obvious reasons not many have received publicity—where citizens who have offended the party in power were suddenly visited by agents of the Bureau and subjected to interrogation and examination. Of course, the Bureau is entirely within its legal right to do so, and there is no proof that the citizens' views prompted these special investigations. It cannot be proved that the purpose was to silence opposition. But the practice is so well known that men of means have scrupulously avoided involvement in movements critical of the Administration, even though privately they are in sympathy with such movements.

The corruption of freedom on the individual level is bad enough. But the corruption of freedom on a mass scale is worse. When the political establishment undertakes to undermine the integrity of the people as a whole, to weaken their power of resistance to authority, and even to lure them into an acceptance of it, then freedom has no leg to stand on. This is exactly what income taxation does, particularly with its exemption device. Bribery through exemption is a most insidious form of corruption.

The Civil War income-tax laws did not exempt churches or educational institutions. While it seems that the government did not get much revenue from them, churchmen and educators had no special reason to support income taxation. They did not like it any more than did other citizens. Whether or not the later advocates of income taxation recalled this fact is not known; but they did advertise it around, when the Amendment was under consideration, that the proposed law would exempt the incomes of institutions "not operated for profit." Furthermore, they promised, the law would permit contributors to such institutions to deduct donations from their taxable incomes. Clergy and educators were quick to see that this privilege would give them an advantage in soliciting contributions, an advantage that gave rise to the slogan: "You might as well give it to us as to the government." Income taxation thus won over a large body of opinion formers. *They were bribed into support of an immoral law.*

Before 1913, economics textbooks did not make much of the ability-to-pay doctrine. Some professors did advocate taxes on corporations, for revenue purposes, but only the few avowed socialists among them ventured to advocate "taxation for social purposes." Today, *practically every textbook used in our college economics courses proclaims the virtue*

72

of progressive income taxation as a means of "distributing wealth." Whether the exemption privilege enjoyed by the colleges had anything to do with this change of thought, it would be impossible to prove; but the inference is justified.

And now that income taxation has reached the point that contributors to colleges cannot be as liberal as they used to be, and the colleges are finding it difficult to meet their expenses, there is a great tendency to look to the government for subsidies. Many educators are concerned lest their cherished "academic freedom" suffer from government intervention. Nevertheless, the prevailing attitude among educators toward Big Government—and therefore heavier taxes—is more than favorable, and one wonders whether this attitude is influenced by the need of the colleges for funds. And one cannot help wondering whether the economics textbooks produced since 1913 would have found so much good in income taxation—and so much bad in private property—if these institutions had not been singled out for special favor.

In 1946, the artifice of bribery through exemption was linked to a law to regulate lobbying. This law requires citizens or groups who are engaged in attempting to influence legislation to register with the government. The corollary of this law is that registered lobbying organizations cannot enjoy tax exemption under the "nonprofit" provision of the income-tax law; it is interesting to note that religious bodies which maintain lobbying committees in Washington do not have to register, and therefore do not jeopardize their tax-exempt status.

The effect of this registration law was not to reduce the practice of lobbying—in fact, lobbying has become an important business—but to intimidate the directors of foundations;

73

for fear that they might lose their tax-exemption privilege by supporting any movement that even by indirection might be called "political," or by "attempting to influence legislation," they are most scrupulous in examining applications for donations. They must give money only to "educational" ventures—as if education were free from ideological bias. Thus, *the so-called lobbying law has had the effect of bribing Americans into abandoning their right of protest.* ·

In 1950, the ruling regime made an attempt to press this lobbying law against several organizations attempting to influence thought unpleasant to the Administration. The government set up a Congressional committee° to investigate all lobbying activities, *but by odd coincidence this committee selected for study only a few that were distributing anticollectivistic and pro-limited-government literature.*

The committee began its "investigation" by redefining lobbying; it asserted that any "substantial effort"—meaning any effort backed with some money—to influence thought that might even indirectly influence legislation must come under the head of "lobbying"; those behind any such effort should register. Since the organizations selected for scrutiny enjoyed the tax-exempt privilege, this meant, if the committee had its way, a loss of revenue; the supporters of these organizations could not deduct their contributions for tax purposes. The committee went on to demand of these organi-

° The notorious Buchanan Committee. Edward A. Rumely, executive secretary of the Committee for Constitutional Government, was cited for contempt of Congress, and sentenced to jail, for refusing to give this committee a list of the buyers of its publications. He was finally exonerated in a higher court; but the cost of litigation, plus the losses sustained by cancellation of book orders from frightened buyers, came to $150,000, he reported. The Buchanan Committee achieved its purpose of reducing the revenues of a dissident organization.

zations a list of their contributors; this insistence on disclosure had only one purpose, that of intimidating and harassing citizens who supported organizations the Administration did not like. Though nothing came of the work of this committee, for political reasons, the point was driven home that organizations enjoying tax exemption had better be careful.

The corruption of freedom is in proportion to the moral deterioration of the people. For a people who have lost their sense of self-respect have no need for freedom. And the income tax, by transferring the property of earners to the State, has disintegrated the moral fiber of Americans to such a degree that they do not even recognize the fact.

Due to the revenues from income taxation, the government is now the largest employer in the country, the largest financier, the largest buyer of goods and services; and, of course, the largest eleemosynary institution. Millions of people are dependent upon it for a livelihood. They lean upon the State, the one propertied "person," even as a bonded servant leans upon his master. They demand doles and subsidies from it, and willingly exchange their conscience (as at the ballot booth) for the gift of sustenance. Wardship under the State, by way of unemployment insurance, public housing, gratuities for not producing, and bounties of one kind or another, has become the normal way of getting along; and in this habit of accepting and expecting handouts, the pride of personality is lost.

Because abolition of income taxes would undermine the value of the government bonds in the banker's vaults, would do away with the subventions by which manufacturers and

75

farmers thrive, would force into productive work the millions who now feed at the public trough, would lessen the special benefits ex-soldiers would expect—who would be for abolition? Socialism has a way of corroding human dignity.

Moral deterioration is a progressive process. Just as a worn part of a machine will affect contiguous parts and finally destroy the entire mechanism, so the loss of one moral value must ultimately undermine the sense of morality.

The income tax, by attacking the dignity of the individual at the very base, has led to the practice of perjury, fraud, deception, and bribery. Avoidance or evasion of the levies has become the great American game, and talents of the highest order are employed in the effort to save something from the clutches of the State. People who in their private lives are above reproach will resort to the meanest devices to effect some saving and will even brag of their ingenuity. The necessity of trying to get along under the income tax has made us a corrupt people.

CHAPTER VIII

A Possible Way Out

THE AMERICAN brand of socialism known as the New Deal was made possible by the income tax. But with the advent of income taxation, socialism was unavoidable.

There have always been, and perhaps always will be, people who are averse to letting other people alone. Recognizing the human inclination to err, they are impelled by their kindness of heart to overcome this imperfection; invariably they come up with a sure-proof plan that needs only political power to become effective. Political power is the essential ingredient of every one of these plans to improve the human.

Since all the ills of mankind, they argue, follow from the exercise of free will, it follows that the only cure for these ills is to suppress free will and to compel the individual to behave in all things as per the perfect pattern devised by these improvers. Compulsion means force; there must be a policeman to see that the individual does not follow his own inclinations.

But policemen must live. Since they do not produce a thing by which they can live, others must support them. Hence, the planners must have the means of getting at the production of the very people who are to be improved by the policeman. That means taxes, and the more taxes the greater the number of enforcement agents, and therefore the more comprehensive the plan. *No plan can be bigger than its bureaucracy.*

The income tax is the ideal instrument for the planner. It not only enables him to exercise his imagination to the last dollar that can be taken from the producers—for their own improvement, of course—but it also weakens the will to resist the plan. The less property the individual has at his disposal, the less room there is for the exercise of his will. He must conform as a matter of necessity. That is to say, *social power decreases as political power increases.*

The income tax was put upon us in 1913. But the improvers of mankind could do little with it for a long time, for the tradition of freedom still held the American in its grip; and the improvers were confined to expounding theories in their papers, or haranguing crowds from a soapbox.

World War I, with its tremendous costs, opened up the door a little; the politician acquired the habit of increasing the levies, and a few regulators of society were pulled in by the draught. It was not until the depression of 1929 that the opportunity to remake American presented itself. This was the opportunity long hoped for. The distress caused by the depression made a shambles of the tradition of freedom; hunger, and the fear of it, have a way of wiping out the value of everything but food. Americans were willing to forget everything they had prized for centuries in exchange for even the promise of an improved economy. The planners were ready with promises. They never made good, of course, and finally had to resort to war to stir up some economic activity; but they had acquired power, and that was all that counted.

If it had not been Mr. Roosevelt and his horde of self-seeking visionaries, it would have been somebody else. The New Deal, or something like it, was planted when the Sixteenth Amendment was put into the Constitution. It needed only the fertilization of the depression to bring it to flower. Whatever politician happened to be at the helm at the propitious moment would have done more or less what Mr. Roosevelt did. That is because *the business he is in, politics, drives the politician toward the acquisition of more and more power, and a good politician is one who takes advantage of every contingency to increase his power.* Mr. Roosevelt was an excellent politician.

Once socialism gets hold of a country, there seems to be nothing that will pry it loose except a complete collapse of the political setup, either as the result of a disastrous war or by way of revolution. The revolutionary way is the least promising, simply because under socialism the will to resist weakens in proportion to the people's adjustment to regulation, control, and domination. Because that is the only way to rub along, they make peace with the conditions imposed on them; they lose the habit of self-respect.

Thus, in this country it has become quite proper for bankers and industrialists to stand in the Washington line with "tin cups" in their hands, for veterans and the unemployed to press for handouts, for farmers to expect subsidies, for the educational fraternity and the ministry to maintain bounty-begging lobbies. All this is the regular order of things; freedom, which demands self-reliance, is out of style. If the miraculous politician should come along, and urge that all this paternalism should be abandoned, as well as

79

the income tax, he would probably receive short shrift from the public.

Even if the politicians should sidestep a war—one that would decimate the population and destroy the economy—what is the next step toward which socialism leads? Communism. The purpose of socialism is to put control of society in the hands of government through control of its economy. But if individuals persist in trying to circumvent the political establishment, say by establishing "black" markets, or if they preach doctrines inimical to the interest of the ruling group, then it follows that freedom of all kinds, most particularly freedom of thought, must be suppressed. That is communism.

The transition from partial to complete socialism, from the New Deal to communism, will not be easy in this country, because the phrases of freedom still sound sweet to us. Given a state of war, or a constant threat of war, or even another depression, and the memories would be obliterated; *we will ask for a savior and we will get communism.* It will not be exactly what the Russians have; it will be an American version.

Is there no hope? Cannot America, the greatest experiment in free government in the history of the world, be saved from the fate that socialism is preparing for her?

It so happens that when this country was organized, the Founding Fathers, either by design or as a matter of necessity, effected an arrangement that is a road block to complete socialization. That is the division of authority between the several states and the federal government. This separation gave rise to the doctrine of States' Rights. The following

80

chapters of this book will attempt to show how this doctrine can be employed to prevent the coming of complete socialism, or absolutism, to this country. Of course, the doctrine will have to be implemented with a will to repeal the Sixteenth Amendment; but that will can be generated, simply because it is to the interests of the forty-eight political establishments that this Amendment be repealed.

CHAPTER IX

Competition in Government

THE AMERICAN political terrain, so to speak, is most favorable for a fight for freedom. The tradition of home rule, supported by the constitutional doctrine of States' Rights, presents a formidable obstacle, if properly exploited, to the forces of collectivism. We have their own admission to that fact.

Early in the socialistic New Deal, its leaders recognized in the division of authority between state and federal governments a difficult impediment to their plans. They set their minds on overcoming it. They went so far as to draw up a blueprint for an arrangement that would circumvent, if not obliterate, the troublesome state lines. In 1940, Mr. Roosevelt's National Resources Committee, in a report called *Regional Factors in National Planning*, proposed that the nation be divided into a dozen regional areas, as a basis for the coordination of federal administrative services. Recognizing that what they proposed was actually violative of the Constitution, they hastened to give assurance: the regional system, they said, "should not be considered a new form of sovereignty, not even in embryo." It would have been foolish to say anything else, since the consolidation of the states into a national unit requires, under the Constitution, the joint action of Congress and the state legislatures. Nevertheless, the report was a bid for a nationalized system, pure and simple. The committee insisted that so long as the "division of constitutional powers remained," the government is handicapped in handling "national problems." In those days the inspired propaganda insisted that the states were "finished."

Thus, the collectivists are on record as to their tactical campaign: the separate states must be wiped out or reduced to parish status. Later, they veered from a direct frontal attack on our traditional system, and went in for liquidation of state autonomy by bribery of state officials.

When you dig down to the psychology of our States' Rights tradition you see the soundness of the collectivists' tactics. The legal difficulties that the division of authority presents is not their main trouble; these can be circumvented by new laws, political deals, and judicial interpretations.* The real obstacle is the psychological resistance to centralization that the States' Rights tradition fosters. The citizen of divided allegiance cannot be reduced to subservi-

---

* One device for invading the authority of the states, under cover of the "general welfare," is the establishment of "authorities," of which the Tennessee Valley Authority is the prototype. Putting aside the economic desirability of these agencies, or their ability to do a job that might be better done by private industry, they are a distinct threat to the autonomy of the states. They are, in fact, "authorities," in that the land they occupy, which is extensive, is federal land and under the jurisdiction of Washington. They are politically alienated from the states. The states, of course, collect no *taxes* from the federal government, and they also lose the revenue that the private users of this land once paid to them. (The TVA generously makes a "donation" to the states, in lieu of the lost taxes.)

83

ence; if he is in the habit of serving two political gods he cannot be dominated by either one.

History supports the argument. No political authority ever achieved absolutism until the people were deprived of a choice of loyalties. It was because the early Christians put God above Caesar that they were persecuted, even though they paid homage and taxes to the established political establishment. Stalin's liquidation of the religious and fraternal orders followed from his basic premise that the Soviet was the only deity. Mussolini was always bothered by the hold the Catholic Church had on the people, and Stalin would never have been Stalin if he had not brought the orthodox church to foot. And so, if the Californian thinks of himself as a Californian as well as an American, and has two flags to support his contention, the central authority rests on shifting ground.*

In no country where centralism got going did the regime have to contend with divided authority such as our Constitution provides. Long before Hitler came on the scene, Bismarck had liquidated the autonomous German states. Mussolini's march on Rome would not have gotten started in the nineteenth century when Italy was an aggregation

---

* To the early American his state government was at least on a par with the federal government in his esteem. Illustrative is the following incident: President Washington was about to arrive at Boston on a visit, and Governor Hancock was perturbed over a matter of protocol; would he be compromising the dignity of the Commonwealth of Massachusetts if he went to meet the "father of his country" on arrival, or would it be more proper that the President call at the state Capitol? The Governor finally settled the problem by pleading illness. . . . The sequel to that incident is worth noting. President Washington was asked to review the Massachusetts militia; he refused on the ground that the militia was the military arm of the state, not the federal government; after all, the tacit understanding in those days was that the militia might be called upon to face the federal army.

of independent units. And, of course, the Czars handed Lenin a thoroughly centralized government.

In this country, the advocates of centralism have had hard going because of our entrenched tradition of States' Rights. It is a tradition that is older than the Constitution, older than the Revolution. It is a national birthmark.

The people of the recently liberated British colonies had had their fill of unlimited government. If they were going to have any national government at all it would have to be quite different from the one they had kicked out. They would put their trust in a government of neighbors, for that kind of establishment could be watched and handled. They were for Union, of course, for by Union they had done away with the foreign tyrant, and they wanted something that would correct the imperfections in the Union they had. They sent delegates to the Philadelphia Convention to correct these imperfections. But they did not want Union at the cost of government resembling in the least that which they had discarded.

When the Convention came out with a brand-new Constitution, not improved Articles of Confederation, as expected, the people were suspicious of it. Ratification of the Constitution came hard, and was not effected without some sharp political practices. In the antiratification literature of the day, long buried by federalist historians, the main theme was that the proposed government might intervene in local affairs and in their private affairs. Their touchiness on that point is reflected in the very composition of the Constitution. The Founding Fathers were very careful to make clear that the new federal government would

85

have certain specified powers, and nothing more.* Whatever powers were not enumerated in the Constitution would remain with the states. No other kind of Constitution could have got by.

One must go to pre-Revolutionary history for the legal origins of States' Rights, but it is sufficient for the present argument to show that it is an essential Americanism, a bit of folklore learned at the nation's cradles. Both the Founding Fathers and the opponents of the Constitution were agreed on the principle of divided authority as a safeguard of the rights of the individual. No one (except a few monarchists) questioned that. The only question was whether the separation was definite enough. It is unfortunate that the doctrine of States' Rights has become sullied with sectionalism and racism, and its original meaning lost in the bitterness of other issues. Perhaps the name should be dropped in favor of "home rule"; but the essential point, that *divided authority is the bulwark of freedom,* is still sound Americanism, and ought to be exploited to the full. It can be invoked in a fight to repeal the Sixteenth Amendment.

But why is the case of freedom stronger when the autonomy of the states is inviolate? There is no vice in the national

*In number 45 of *The Federalist*, Madison writes: "The powers delegated by the proposed Constitution to the federal government are few and defined. Those which remain in the state governments are numerous and indefinite. The former will be exercised principally on external objects, as war, peace, negotiation and foreign commerce. . . . The powers reserved to the several states will extend to all objects which, in the ordinary course of affairs, concern the lives, liberties and properties of the people, and the internal order, improvement and prosperity of the state." And so *The Federalist* goes on; promise after promise that the state governments will be free in all respects except to deal with foreign governments. At one time, Madison described the federal government as the foreign department for the state governments.

government that cannot be duplicated in the government of a subdivision; even county sheriffs have been known to take liberties with the rights of citizens. If we were living in forty-eight separate nations our lot, as individuals, might be worse; it probably would. Some people, using Switzerland as example, maintain that the smaller the nation the more freedom. But the Central American dictatorships refute that argument. The characteristic of the Swiss government that is often overlooked is the division of authority between the federal establishments and the cantons. That is the essential ingredient: only when the central authority is kept off balance by competition from autonomous subdivisions are the rights of citizens more secure.

Freedom is the absence of restraint. Government cannot give freedom, it can only take it away. The more power the government exercises the less freedom will the people enjoy. And when government has a monopoly of power the people have no freedom. That is the definition of absolutism —monopoly of power.

The object of monopoly, in any field, is to compel the customer to accept the services offered by the monopolist at his own terms. It is a take-it-or-leave-it arrangement. Competition, on the other hand, compels the servicer to meet the standards set by his competitors, with the customer the final judge as to proficiency. The beneficiary of competition is the buyer. In the matter of government services— which is the protection of life and property—the customer is the citizen.° The government will serve him best only if it

---

° "The first object of government," says Madison in the tenth number of *The Federalist*, is the protection of "the diversity in the faculties of men, from which the rights of private property originate." The conception of

cannot set its own standards, when it does not enjoy a complete monopoly of power.

This brings up a contradiction. The theory is that government must have a monopoly of coercion to prevent us from using coercion indiscriminately on one another; we institute government, and endow it with sole police power, for the purpose of maintaining order. Nevertheless, experience has shown that the monopoly we give government can work for disorder; the power can be used to create disharmony and promote injustice. That, in fact, is the record. *Throughout history, those to whom the job of rulership has fallen, whether by heredity or popular selection, have shown a tendency to use their position to dominate, not serve, the ruled.* Hence, unless the monopoly of power can be checkmated, freedom is always in danger.

Recognition of that fact gave rise to the idea of constitutional government, with limited powers. And as further restraint on government, popular suffrage was instituted. The vote is presumed to keep the government from getting out of hand; the threat of being turned out at the next election is supposed to hold down the arrogance and ambition of those in whom the power is vested. However, during its incumbency the elected government does enjoy a monopoly position, and it can use that position to solidify, enlarge upon, and perpetuate its power; it can even use the citizens' tax money to "buy up" the next election, either by bribery or by propaganda.

Popular suffrage is in itself no guarantee of freedom. People can vote themselves into slavery.

government held by the Founding Fathers was quite the opposite of what has been gaining currency in this country in recent years.

The only way, then, to prevent the monopoly of power from becoming absolute is to create a competitive market for government; to give the citizens, the customers, a choice of jurisdiction. That is exactly what our peculiar American system of divided authority, between states and federal government, accomplished. The Constitution, as originally conceived, set up independent nations within an independent nation—*imperium in imperio*—each with delimited powers. In that way, it was hoped, the polarization of power that undermines freedom would be prevented. The central government was given certain specified chores to do; it could not intervene in local affairs, unless the state governments were not able to maintain order. If the state government got rough with its customers, they could easily transfer their allegiance to another state.

This division of powers established the nearest thing to competition in government the world has ever known. As long as it held up, or until the federal government invaded the state lines (through the powers it acquired under the Sixteenth Amendment), the American citizen was as free as it is possible to be in organized society. Except with excise taxes, or during war, the central government never annoyed him. Sometimes the state governments went in for political innovations, including socialism, that violated his freedom. But they did not get far with these schemes, simply because the citizen could march off to a state more to his liking, or immigration from other states was discouraged; no government likes to lose taxpayers.

Thus, before the Prohibition Amendment, several states and localities went in for this kind of sumptuary legislation. This was indeed an invasion of individual rights, but it never

89

amounted to much more than a nuisance. There was no monopoly of power behind it. The citizen could and did import liquor from contiguous territory, or manufactured his own. Until the prohibitory power was monopolized by the federal government, so that escape was fraught with danger, the individual's right to make a drunken fool of himself was not effectively infringed by state laws.

From the very beginning the states had the power to impose income taxes and a number of them exercised it. None of these states ever went as far as the federal government has gone, and for obvious reasons. In the first place, the neighborly relations between local tax collectors and taxpayers made for evasion of this infringement of property rights; the state governments could not import "foreigners" from Washington to do the unpleasant work. Then, the local politician is more sensitive to the likelihood of retribution at the polls than is the national politician, and he knows that nothing will stir up the people more violently than excessive taxation. Most important is the fact that, other things being equal, capital, without which production is impossible, is attracted to areas where low tax rates obtain; it was regular practice, before the Sixteenth Amendment, for chambers of commerce to advertise the freedom from income taxes in their states as an enticement to industry, and it was not unusual for men of means to migrate to those states that did not tax inheritances. Running away from taxes is an ancient custom, and no state government wants to see its area depopulated. For these reasons some of the states dropped their income taxes, and none of them went in for oppressive rates.

Sometimes it is urged that we federalize our divorce laws, which would indeed be an invasion of our personal lives.

So long as there are different legal jurisdictions covering divorce, the morality of it is left where it should be, in the conscience of the parties involved. A federal law would not prevent the breaking of conjugal ties, but if it were stringent enough it would certainly encourage the practice of living together out of wedlock, with a consequent increase of illegitimacy. Thus, immorality would be multiplied, as every law to eradicate it does. The more affluent would migrate to other countries to effect their purpose. More important, from the viewpoint of freedom, a federal law would put upon us another flock of enforcement agents, snoopers, and bribe takers.

Right now there is an urgency to have the federal government eradicate by forcible means the stupidity of racial and religious bigotry, particularly in employment practices. This is another example of the fatuous undertaking to make men "good" by law—the socialistic program. It cannot be done. A "fair employment practices" law can only result in intensifying bigotry, by concentrating attention on it. A New York State law of that kind has done nothing more than stimulate the ingenuity of employers and employment agencies to invent methods of evasion; discrimination is as prevalent as ever. But if the federal government is given the power of a "fair employment practices" act, we can expect an army or corruptible police swarming all over our national industry. That is not freedom.

As long as anything is left of our tradition of States' Rights, the danger of absolutism in this country can be avoided. In fact, it is that tradition that must be depended upon in any effort to repeal the Sixteenth Amendment.

CHAPTER X

Union Forever

THE CIVIL WAR did not abolish the autonomy of the
states. All that was settled by that conflict was the questions
of secession and nullification; no state could pull out of the
Union or disregard a regularly enacted national law. After
1865, as before, the states were still the depositories of all
powers not specifically delegated to the federal government,
as stipulated in the Constitution.

*After 1913, however, and without either a war or a change
in the law of the land, the states were gradually and almost
imperceptibly rid of their sovereign position and reduced in
importance to dependent subdivisions of the nation. It was
done by the subtle arts of bribery and blackmail, made possible by the Sixteenth Amendment.*

From the very beginning of the Union it has been customary for Congressmen to try to wangle out of the federal
government some special privilege for their more influential
supporters, or some appropriation of federal funds for spending in their states. "Pork barrel" legislation did not begin
with the Sixteenth Amendment. However, before 1913 the
best the party in power could do for a Congressman (or a
state governor), by way of a bribe, was to let him hand out a

92

judgeship or a postmastership, an occasional franchise or perhaps a land grant.° Such favors helped the state machines to see eye to eye with the federal government and win their support for its programs; but the total of such patronage was not enough to reduce the states to subserviency. The manna that fell from Washington was hardly enough to buy up the independence of the states or the votes of their citizens. No candidate for Congress could offer his constituents gifts paid for by the citizens of other states.

The ink was hardly dry on the Sixteenth Amendment before the heretofore picayune federal patronage began to blossom into the program of grants-in-aid. The first of these came in 1914, when the Agricultural Extension Service was inaugurated with an appropriation of $480,000—not so inconsiderable an amount in those days. Each year thereafter Congress found reason to pass "general welfare" legislation, with appropriations increasing in importance. Whether the "general welfare" prospered by these expenditures is questionable, but it is certain that the political fortunes of the politicians who could boast of "bringing home the bacon" did not suffer.

The laws multiplied and the appropriations grew bigger. It is a curious fact that as the government's revenues increase so do its needs.

Before 1913, the country was in difficulty several times,

° During recent years, the federal government has regained by purchase or state grant a good portion of the land it so lavishly distributed for political purposes during the nineteenth century. It now owns about one fourth of the land of the country. Since this is federal land, the states cannot collect any taxes from its users. This is practically "foreign soil" as far as the states are concerned, outside their jurisdiction and yielding them no land tax.

but it never suffered from an "emergency"; that national disease is a product of the income tax, and as the levies increased, the affliction recurred with greater frequency and greater intensity.

War, or the threat of it, is a most important "emergency," and since 1913 we have had two major wars, a "punitive expedition" and at least one "police action." We finally got around to permanent peacetime conscription, thanks to an "emergency," with its costs. In between all this a depression came upon us, even as did "hard times" several times before the Sixteenth Amendment. The country managed to get out of these former economic disasters without federal intervention; but the depression of 1929 was not allowed to cure itself; it had to be ministered to with taxes.

Every post-Sixteenth Amendment "emergency" became an occasion for raising the rates of taxes on incomes and of lowering the exemptions; that is, for taking more of the incomes of more persons. *The odd thing about these "emergency" taxes is that they hang on after the original occasion for them disappears.* Just by way of illustration, first-class postage before World War II was two cents an ounce; the rate was raised to three cents "for the duration." Later legislation made the increase permanent. Perhaps other factors, like inflation, made continuation of the increased rate necessary, although that is a debatable question; the point is that the promise of the original legislation was never kept. In like manner, a great "need" ushered in every increase in income taxes, with the tacit or explicit understanding that the levies would be dropped when the "need" no longer existed; but every "need" hardened into a permanent necessity.

Popular suffrage fosters government by and for pressure

groups. *The first concern of a politician is to be elected, the second is to be reelected.* No matter how noble he is at heart, no matter how sincere his desire to serve his country, practical considerations force him to cater to individuals or groups who can "deliver the vote"; he cannot do anything for the good of his country unless he is in office. Hence, he is inclined to make promises to do this or that for the benefit of those who can help him at the polls. Since an office holder has nothing to offer but laws, his preelection promises amount to the pledging of the political power with which he is invested. But the patriotic citizens who enter into the bargain are not interested in political power in itself; what they are after is an economic advantage that political power can confer upon them. They are interested in sinecures on the public payroll, franchises, public works and contracts that bring jobs to the community and profits for the contractors, handouts, and so on.

This practice of buying votes with political favors is inherent in popular government. It is the weakness of democracy. It is not due so much to the depravity of the politician as to the human hunger for something-for-nothing.

However, this weakness of democracy is only as dangerous as the amount of the citizens' wealth the government has at its disposal. Before 1913 the American government was comparatively poor and political jobbery was correspondingly limited in scope. When the government acquired this power of confiscating the national wealth, the corruption was limited only by the amount that expediency would permit it to confiscate. At this writing the confiscation amounts to one third of the production of the citizenry. That is a lot of "pork" with which to buy votes. And so, as the

95

Sixteenth Amendment gradually achieved its fulfillment, the politician's attention was more and more directed toward the "barrel"; so was the attention of those who are compelled to keep it filled.

The dependence of the state political machinery on the coffers of the federal government carries an obligation: to support and acquiesce in the policies and purposes of the ruling regime. If a governor asks for or accepts a school subvention, he cannot very well object to the curriculum or textbooks "recommended" by the Bureau of Education. And a Congressman who tries to become a liaison officer between his voters and the United States Treasury will probably vote for any program the regime wants. Even a city mayor might find it politically inexpedient to reject a housing subsidy offered by the federal government. The funds at the disposal of Washington make it possible for the bureaucracy to go over the heads of noncooperative local politicians to the people, to propagandize them in favor of what it wants and against the independent local politician; it is a known fact that the Washington bureaucracy maintains a most extensive propaganda machine.

Thus, every federal dollar spent in a state becomes an obligation on the state. The obligation is paid off with sovereignty; the state sells out its independence. It is all done without change of the law, without any modification of the Constitution, and is as imperceptible as the gradual wearing down of a proud horse by a resolute trainer.

Once in a while, however, the fact of what is going on is dramatically disclosed when a state government asserts its independence. Thus, when the Indiana legislature, during the Truman administration, decided to make public its relief rolls, in order to put a stop to corruption in the distribution of public money, the federal government showed its fangs; it threatened to withdraw its fifty percent contribution to these relief funds if Indiana persisted in its purpose. This blatant attack on the sovereignty of a member of the Union received wide publicity. It will probably never be known how much quiet pressure is put on state governments (through favors extended to local politicians) to submit to federal domination.

This centralization of power, which the Founding Fathers feared and sought to prevent by constitutional safeguards, is made possible only by income taxation. This is the atomic bomb that has virtually destroyed the Union. But, it may be pointed out, the state legislatures ratified the Sixteenth Amendment in the first place; did they not know that they were voting themselves out of business? Probably not. Most of the states were poor and envious of those in better circumstances, and all they saw in the Sixteenth Amendment was a way to "soak the rich."

For some years after the Amendment went into effect, seven states of the Union paid in more to the federal government in income taxes than they got back in the form of grants-in-aid; the other forty-one made a "profit." Covetousness was thus encouraged. Somehow, a Mississippian sees no immorality in forcing a Pennsylvanian to support his local economy. His pride might stop him from accepting a gratuity from his neighbor, but he suffers no such inhibition when he knows it comes from a "foreigner." So, it came to pass that a Congressional coalition, representing the poorer states, and held together only by their common greed, pressed for legislation that would bring them dollars mulcted

97

mainly from the citizens of the seven rich states. That is the bald fact, though the legislation was glamorized with the "public interest" label. According to the label, New York profits by its forced contribution to Arizona irrigation projects or Montana roads. However that might be, the immediate beneficiary of federal grants to local projects is the politician who solicits it, and the ultimate beneficiary is the federal bureaucracy. Everybody else pays.

Today, every state in the Union pays into the income-tax fund more than it gets back. (See table at the end of this chapter.) This outcome was inevitable. The Sixteenth Amendment gives the federal government power to levy on incomes "from any source derived." This includes the incomes of citizens in the poorer states, and the federal . government had to get around to them in time.

But the fact that every state is now a loser gives them all a common interest in the repeal of the Amendment. They all have an economic motive for raising the banner of States' Rights, for reestablishing their sovereignty; they would all profit by repeal of income taxation. How could they lose?

Twice in the history of the country the doctrine of home rule was called from retirement to lead a secessionist movement, and each time the motivation was economic. In 1814, when the British fleet had all but ruined New England industry and commerce, delegates from these states met to consider ways and means, not excluding secession from the Union. What might have come from the Hartford Convention must remain conjecture, for "Mr. Madison's War" was called off before the proposed second gathering was con-

98

vened. The renewal of business activity put the doctrine back into the textbooks.

States' Rights became the battle cry of the South only because the planters felt the pinch of protective tariffs. No one would ever have heard of nullification and secession, and certainly not of war, if Calhoun's plea for lower tariffs had been heeded—or if the government had been able to buy off the planters with "parity" prices, which it could not do for lack of an income tax. After the war had destroyed the economic interest which had inspired it, States' Rights was again interred.

The fires of freedom are stoked by the will to be free. It is not the promise of bread alone that will spur a people to shed their shackles, but rather the hope that they may attain the dignity of self-respecting individuals. Without idealism a revolution is nothing but a gang fight. Nevertheless, it will be found that every struggle for freedom was led by a group who, though prompted by lofty purposes, had some immediate economic objective in mind; it may not have been personal gain that drove them to act, it may have been the improvement of general conditions, but in any case an economic motivation was present. Nor will the rank-and-file go through the struggle of liberation unless they can see a pot of gold in the rainbow.

At the present time there is no economic group sufficiently disturbed about income taxation to start doing something about it. On the other hand, a sizable number of Americans, and particularly those who have the resourcefulness to take care of themselves under any conditions, have managed to attach themselves to the income-tax wagon and see no reason for breaking it up.* They are doing pretty well for themselves, so well, in fact, that they are blinded to the ultimate effects of income taxation on the welfare of their offspring, on the future of their country. To them the income tax has been good.

For instance, the banking fraternity is not overly disturbed by high income taxation; because of these revenues, the government can guarantee the mortgages the banks hold on overvalued veterans' homes and other housing projects; these guarantees might not be worth much if the Sixteenth Amendment were repealed.† The industrialists who revel in a backlog of government orders likewise see no reason for repeal. Nor can the farmers work up any interest in the

---

* A striking instance of how the federal government has built up a vested interest in income taxes is the case of the Reconstruction Finance Corporation. This agency, set up in the Hoover Administration on a "temporary" basis, makes loans to companies who can prove that private financial institutions have rejected their applications; that is, to companies that are not entitled, on the basis of their financial statements or their performance, to loans Some 14,000 of such presumably unsafe companies, in 1950, had obtained funds from the RFC, the citizens of the United States were compelled to loan money to people whom the banks had turned down. Obviously, the borrowers were grateful. The Sixteenth Amendment was very good to them. Since this was written, Congress has terminated the life of the RFC, and has replaced it with the Small Business Loan Corporation.

† The condition of the banks is worth commenting upon, because of the importance of these institutions to the general economy. The banks, as a whole, now hold government bonds in an amount equal to upwards of sixty percent of their total assets. A sizable drop in the value of these bonds could wipe out their net worth and bring on an insolvent position. Repeal of income taxation would certainly affect the value of these bonds adversely. The banks must be against it. Furthermore, they are in the peculiar position of not being able to refuse to take more bonds, because such refusal would be tantamount to repudiating the soundness of their main borrower, and thus casting reflection on their own soundness. Thus, the banks have slipped into the position of dependence on and subservience to the United States Treasury; to all intents and purposes they constitute the bank of the government.

matter, since it is out of income-tax revenues that they get "parity" support as well as checks for not producing. College professors whose salaries depend on government subsidies, veterans whose incomes are augmented by gratuities from the federal treasury, dentists who pull teeth at government expense, tenants whose rent is more or less paid by the government, two and a half million who are on the public payroll—probably half the population of America are wholly or in part dependent on income taxes for their livelihood, have made a comfortable adjustment with it, and though they grumble about the part they have to pay, would not like to have their adjustment disturbed.

Among these beneficiaries of the income tax are the type of people who could be the backbone of a revolt. In time, they will be, for it cannot be long before their benefits will be more than offset by the taxes they have to pay; the "take" of the government, increasing as a percentage, must ultimately wipe out the winnings of all the players. When that time comes, or when they become aware of it, those who are now for income taxation will discover that they have been robbed not only of their property but also of their freedom, and will kick up a fuss. Meanwhile, they are content to keep their snouts in the public trough.

That part of the population who get no return on their income-tax payments—obviously, the government cannot subsidize everybody—are too preoccupied with the problem of making ends meet to do anything but grumble. Were a leadership to appear, explaining that repeal of the Sixteenth Amendment would do away with withholding taxes, that the waitress would not have to share her tips with the tax collector, that the grocer would no longer have to hire

101

an accountant to keep him out of jail, that the housewife would not have to conspire with her housemaid to evade the law, a goodly crowd would join up.

The only group that could logically furnish that leadership are the governors and legislators of the states. Repeal of federal income taxes would not only reestablish their importance and dignity, but would also put them in the way of increasing the revenues of the states for the carrying on of such social services as the citizens call for. The states would set themselves up in business again. And some degree of statesmanship could attach to the job of the representative in Washington if he were relieved of the necessity of panhandling.

Besides, any change in the Constitution is still the prerogative of the states. If three quarters of the members of the Union demand an amendment (and repeal would be an amendment), Congress must put it into the works; the signature of the President is not needed. Hence, the initiation must come from the states.

Repeal of the Sixteenth Amendment would amount to secession of the forty-eight states from Washington—and restoration of the Union.

Union Forever

FEDERAL INTERNAL REVENUE COLLECTIONS OF THE UNITED STATES RE-
PORTED FOR THE FISCAL YEAR 1951, COMPARED WITH REPORTED GRANTS-IN-
AID TO STATE AND LOCAL GOVERNMENTS, AND FEDERAL AID PAYMENTS TO
INDIVIDUALS WITHIN THE RESPECTIVE STATES, OTHER THAN GRANTS AND
LOANS, WITH PERCENT OF COLLECTIONS RETURNED TO EACH STATE IN
FISCAL 1951.

TOTAL INTERNAL REVENUE COLLECTIONS, fiscal
1951[1] $51,487,378,963
Returned to State and local governments and as direct pay-
    ments to individuals   4,850,097,620
AVERAGE PERCENT of total collections returned: 9.42%

State	Internal Revenue Collections	Returned to States or Individuals	Percent Returned
Alabama	$ 298,452,466	$126,667,671	42.44
Arizona	106,437,924	32,399,593	30.44
Arkansas	130,984,457	95,575,552	72.96
California	3,558,227,339	346,489,944	9.73
Colorado	353,849,385	77,001,460	21.76
Connecticut	818,038,816	38,958,392	4.76
Delaware	566,957,101	8,349,423	1.47
Florida	467,624,260	107,994,759	23.09
Georgia	497,447,795	141,615,626	28.47
Idaho	91,354,432	32,105,915	35.14
Illinois	4,328,996,624	201,710,885	4.65
Indiana	1,202,616,546	85,093,494	7.08
Iowa	438,239,605	81,521,885	18.58
Kansas	385,361,679	58,214,755	15.10
Kentucky	1,056,514,846	90,585,619	8.57
Louisiana	410,122,482	179,171,766	43.69
Maine	127,370,116	24,580,171	19.29
Maryland[2]	1,417,285,966	140,175,242	9.90
Massachusetts	1,486,571,308	146,442,645	9.80
Michigan	4,156,021,742	144,470,510	3.47
Minnesota	786,759,261	90,239,781	11.47
Mississippi	113,976,845	106,590,440	93.58
Missouri	1,392,271,994	160,044,711	11.50
Montana	91,691,015	34,613,013	35.23
Nebraska	334,020,815	51,135,039	15.31
Nevada	47,505,504	9,670,564	20.36
New Hampshire	87,177,119	14,610,301	16.76
New Jersey	1,460,314,212	85,523,048	5.86
New Mexico	80,607,390	35,819,902	44.44

New York	9,243,924,053	345,822,642	3.74
North Carolina	1,257,159,936	130,988,567	10 42
North Dakota	57,680,073	30,665,635	53.15
Ohio	3,292,928,469	169,122,171	5.13
Oklahoma	494,893,021	117,124,017	23.66
Oregon	361,510,696	53,994,428	14.93
Pensylvania	3,886,470,430	286,116,616	7 36
Rhode Island	239,708,304	21,864,280	9.12
South Carolina	191,326,842	82,551,046	43.14
South Dakota	64,281,915	29,725,521	46.24
Tennessee	398,608,019	140,675,680	35.29
Texas	1,683,259,143	290,169,323	17.24
Utah	109,532,371	34,361,074	31.29
Vermont	48,675,291	11,523,124	23.67
Virginia	863,146,269	65,361,252	7.57
Washington[3]	602,633,864	86,121,485	14.29
West Virginia	245,969,387	46,271,356	18.81
Wisconsin	963,172,326	81,965,115	8.51
Wyoming	48,984,119	23,517,644	48.01
Hawaii	98,022,630	22,478,673	22.93

[1] In 1932 the programs in effect totaled $269,425,252. During the wartime fiscal year 1946, the grants-in-aid and checks to individuals totaled $1,290,107,183. As these figures were compiled, there were 80 programs and activities under which federal revenues were shared with or funneled back to the states and local governments, or as direct payments to individuals. (Payments to individuals were exclusive of payments to civilian employees of the federal government who at this time numbered more than 2,530,000, with payrolls at an annual rate of over $10 billion a year.)

[2] Maryland receipts include revenues from the District of Columbia and Puerto Rico. For fiscal 1951 the District received a total of $34,384,443 in federal aid and Puerto Rico received $54,412,416. The actual Maryland figure is $51,378,383.

[3] Figures on collections for Washington include Alaska. Amounts have not been shown separately by the Treasurer's annual report. Federal aid reported for Alaska for fiscal 1951 totaled $5,789,295.

Author's note: The preliminary summary of this table states that the average percentage of total collections returned to the states and individuals is 9.42. This is an incorrect and misleading figure, and is a perfect example of

104

how easily statistics may be used to state an untruth. It is indeed true that, of the lump sum collected by the federal government from all the states, a *lump-sum percentage* of 9.42 was returned to the states. But it is not true that the *average percentage* returned to each state and individual was 9.42. Actually, the average percentage returned to each state was 22.64. This correct percentage is arrived at by *averaging the 49 percentages* listed in the table.

You can't take 566,957,101 (Delaware), lump it together with 113,976,845 (Mississippi), divide the lump sum into the lump sum of the amounts returned to these two states, then draw an average of the percentages returned to the states. You can't do this because the separate sums are of different amounts, and percentages drawn from two different amounts cannot be averaged. For your average percentages returned to these states, you have to take the two percentages given—1.47 and 93.58—and average them.

CHAPTER XI

For Freedom's Sake

REPEAL OF *the Sixteenth Amendment would not be a reform; it would be a revolution.*

A reform is a procedural change, an alteration in the legal ritual that does not affect the center of political power. A revolution, on the other hand, whether it is effected by violence or in an orderly fashion, is a transference of power from one group to another. An election is in effect a revolution, and so is a *coup d'état* or one of those gang fights that characterize Latin-American politics. The essence of revolution is a shift in the incidence of power.

The significant revolutions of history were those that either strengthened the political establishment or whittled off some of its power. The Bolshevik Revolution of 1917 was a major operation, because it replaced a decadent and weakening Czarism with the most powerful machine the world has ever known; not a shred of social power was left in Russia after the Bolsheviks took over. Then there was the revolution at Runnymede that resulted in the Magna Carta, an instrument that deprived the Crown of some of its prerogatives.

The American Revolution was unique in history, not because it kicked out a foreign rulership, which had been

106

done before, but because it made possible the establishment of a government based on a new and untried principle, namely, that the government has no power except what the governed have granted it. That was a shift in power that had never occurred before.

A new American revolution was initiated in 1913, when the government was invested with the power to confiscate private property. The Amendment was not heralded as a revolution, and very few recognized it as such, but the fact is, as events have shown, that this power over the economy of the country put into the hands of the American government a means of liquidating the sovereignty of the citizenry.

As a result of income taxation, we now have a government with far more power than George III ever exercised. It is self-sufficient, independent of the will of the people. The elections do not alter that fact; these are merely periodic changes of the guard. Whoever is elected retains the power vested in the office and, as usual, tries to augment it. The end in clear sight is the liquidation of all social power and the advent of a regime of absolutism.

This, it cannot too often be repeated, was an inevitable consequence of income taxation. The citizen is sovereign only when he can retain and enjoy the fruits of his labor. If the government has first claim on his property he must learn to genuflect before it. When the right of property is abrogated, all the other rights of the individual are undermined, and to speak of the sovereign citizen who has no absolute right of property is to talk nonsense. It is like saying that the slave is free because he is allowed to do anything he wants to do (even vote, if you wish) except to own what he produces.

107

The proposal to repeal the Sixteenth Amendment is really a proposal to restore the sovereignty of the American citizen. To use a modern term, it is a counterrevolutionary proposal, in that it aims to restore to society the power that the Amendment gave to the government. Judging by the grumbling over income taxes—to say nothing of the wholesale evasion that even the Treasury Department admits—it would seem that the revolutionary tinder box is full and needs only leadership to ignite it. Particularly is this truculence strong among workers and housewives, professional and small businessmen; the big industrialists, bankers, and commercial interests, for the reasons aforementioned, have no reason to favor repeal. But whether this mass dissatisfaction can be channeled into a dynamic movement depends on the underlying cause of it; is it economic or spiritual?

It needs no proving that the country, the people, would be better off if income taxation were abolished. But no movement based on economic grounds alone will stir a people into action; a movement so based can be bought off.

Unless Americans want to be free, unless they put their tradition of freedom above all else, the Sixteenth Amendment will stay in the Constitution until it wrecks both the tradition and the civilization from which it emerged.

It is customary to identify the American tradition with the Declaration of Independence. Yet the Declaration merely articulated what had grown into an American thought pattern long before it was written. It had become the American ethos. John Adams, writing in 1818, put it this way: "the Revolution was in the hearts of men". . . it was effected

108

"before the war commenced." That is to say, when Jefferson wrote about "unalienable rights" he simply put into words what Americans instinctively felt. They opposed the British Crown because they could not do otherwise.

When we try to define "Americanism"—of which there is much loose talk these days—we find it necessary to look to our beginnings for the essential ingredient. Whatever special character this country can lay claim to, it was the habit of freedom that was acquired before the country was formally organized. And it was an acquired, not an inherited characteristic, for the American was ethnologically as heterogeneous as his forebears. His ancestry gave him nothing that the peoples of Europe did not have. He had come by freedom through trouble and toil; he meant to hold on to it.

When he got around to establishing a political establishment of his own, the American had sense enough not to put too much trust in it. He had learned—without the help of a textbook on political science—that inherent in government, any government, is the tendency to rob the individual of his freedom. Hence, while recognizing the need of government for orderly gregarious living, he was against giving any setup a free hand; it must be hamstrung. The Constitution was, for that reason, that distrust of government, heavily underlined with prohibitions and with "checks and balances."

The Constitution was tailor made for and by Americans; it was fitted to their particular habit of thought. That point was emphasized by one of its makers, Gouverneur Morris, when he was Minister to France, during the Reign of Terror. "The French," he wrote, "want an American Constitution

109

without reflecting that they have not American citizens to support it."

Missing from our original Constitution was a "check" that was all the more potent because of its omission. *The straight-thinking pioneer knew full well that the power of the government is in direct ratio to its income, and he was therefore all for cutting its income to the bone; that way it could not get out of hand.* About all he would allow it was what it could pick up from tariffs on imports. Grudgingly, because, as Hamilton pointed out, tariffs could not produce enough to pay the running expenses of the proposed government, he allowed it some excise taxes. More than that he would not give, and more than excise and tariff taxes did not get into the Constitution.

Certainly, no tax on incomes got into the Constitution. That was unthinkable. A people that had but recently kicked over the traces because of taxes far less onerous would hardly have countenanced an income tax. They knew their freedom.

The case for repeal rests on this tradition. If there are still enough Americans who are of the opinion that that government governs best which governs least, if there is among us a group willing to risk their fortunes, their lives, and their sacred honor for freedom, then repeal has a chance. If, on the other hand, the habits of mind acquired under income taxation have completely obliterated the American tradition, then any effort to restore citizen sovereignty is futile.

It is never too late to put up a fight for freedom.

Right now, even in America, the prospect for starting such a fight is unpromising. Not that the goal is unattainable, but that interest in freedom is at so low an ebb. The great enthusiasm of the times is "security"; everybody seems bent on catching this evasive will o' the wisp, oblivious of the fact that it is beyond reach because it does not exist. There is no such thing as "security"; it is a mirage sprouting out of deep-rooted human yearning for something-for-nothing. Government, which lives and thrives on power, fosters belief in the "golden calf," so that it can surreptitiously rob the self-mesmerized worshipers of their wealth and their dignity. It requires no great acumen to realize that what trickles out of the government's cornucopia must be replaced by labor. But reflection is foreclosed by the madness that has come over us. The national passion is for handouts, no matter what the cost. Freedom, which puts a premium on self-reliance, is in short demand. Why put up a fight for it?

The rank and file, those whose principal preoccupation is with the problem of existence, are in no mood to argue with the beneficent State; they are for letting well enough alone. Those Americans who have pretensions to over-average capacities are also quite willing to put their self-esteem on the barrelhead. The entrepreneur whose venture would not exist but for government loans or government contracts readily makes peace with government regulation. So long as government bonds pay interest, the banker will not quarrel with government intervention. The farmer does not object to a meddlesome federal agent who brings him a gratuity, and the professor who lives by subsidies will write books in praise of the subsidizing State.

Who wants freedom?

In the circumstances, those who put a value on freedom,

111

who know that the loss of interest in freedom is the sure mark of national and individual decadence, are in deep despair. Many, too many, have resigned themselves to what they call the inevitable. Let the country have its bellyful of socialism, they say, and be done with the struggle to stop it. The human animal can adjust itself to any condition that permits him a meal and a mate; Americans are no different from any other people that in times past have swapped their souls for a mess of pottage. They, too, will find that the only "security" is that provided by a penal institution, but by the time they find it out they will have made their adjustment to prison bars and barbed wire. After a century or two of that kind of living, some Moses will come along to remind them that they are in fact men, and a new exodus to freedom will be started. By that time, these prophets of gloom maintain, and not without good reason, the State itself will be in a starved condition and unable to stop the exodus. A handful of resolute men will easily topple it over.

There is historic support for such resignation. Every civilization on record has followed the same pattern. In the beginning, the civilization rose and flourished in the sunshine of freedom. And, in the beginning, the civilization was poor. Always some kind of government attached itself to society, but because of the general lack of goods, the government remained quiescent and even rendered service in the maintenance of order.

But the human urge is always away from poverty, and that urge, while it improves his circumstances and widens his horizon, also is man's downfall. As soon as a general abundance appears, the passion for power is enflamed, and the political establishment changes its character; it grad-

112

ually shifts its position from a protective to a predatory institution. It levies taxes. And the more the general economy improves the larger its levies, always, of course, in the "general interest." So it was in the time of the Caesars, so it is now.

The general welfare is not improved by the increasing load of taxation. On the contrary, the upward climb of civilization is retarded in exact proportion to the levies, and when they reach the point of discouraging production, the parabola of civilization turns downward.

Returning to first principles, the object of productive effort is consumption; men work to satisfy their desires, and for no other reason. They don't want work, they want satisfactions. Their aversion to labor is such that they are constantly inventing labor-saving devices. And the more labor they save the more labor they invest in the gratification of new desires, of which the human mind seems to have an inexhaustible fund. Contrariwise, when the results of their efforts are taken from them, when the prospect of possession and enjoyment is diminished, they lose interest in producing. Why work when there is nothing in it? And this disinterest in production arises whether the insecurity of ownership is caused by regular visits from marauders or tax collectors. The name or the uniform of the absconder makes no difference to the one deprived of his property; he sees no point in trying to improve his circumstances, in widening his horizon; his point of interest is mere existence. That is civilization in decline.

When faced with this circumstance, does the State abdicate? It does not. The general lack of interest in production threatens its own existence, but it still cannot divest itself

113

of its inner urge for power. It turns to the use of force to stimulate the production from which it derives taxes. It confiscates and tries to run the entire economy by rules, regulations, controls, and compulsion; the nation becomes a slave-labor camp. But the output of an economy that rests on force rather than on self-interest is meager. More important than lack of production is the slave psychology that such an environment induces. Men lose their capacity for self-improvement along with their sense of individual dignity. Thus civilization disintegrates and becomes an historical or archaeological curio. The State, of course, collapses with the civilization.

Must our civilization follow in the same groove? There are prophets who so maintain. For about three centuries, they point out, that bit of modern civilization called America thrived under the life-giving rays of freedom; now it is entering into the usual regime of absolutism. The end is in sight, and the end, they say, will come much more quickly than did, for instance, the end of the Roman civilization, simply because our great advances in technology will hasten it. We move much faster these days, even toward our decline. The event that will bring about a complete collapse of freedom in America, and the civilization that grew up under it, will be the next world war; the State will, under fear of annihilation from the enemy, confiscate all that remains of social power. After the war, as usual, it will not give up the power it has thus confiscated—in fact, the bewildered and war-impoverished people will insist on the State retaining that power and using it for the "general welfare"—and in short order even the memory of freedom will have been lost.

114

Maybe so. Maybe our civilization must obey the "inelucta-ble" forces of history; maybe it is on the toboggan now. Nevertheless, men do what they are impelled by their natures to do, not by what history dictates. The stars in the heavens attend to their eternal business, while we mortals must travel within our own specific orbits.

It was no historical imperative that directed the pens of those who signed the Declaration of Independence; it was an inner force. There were many at the time—the Tories— who deemed the Revolution a foolhardy venture, from which no good could come greater than that which might ensue from a compromise with King George; if they were alive today these Tories could point to Canada in support of their argument. Nevertheless, the rebels, none of whom were driven to it by economic necessity, put their signatures to what at the time seemed to be their own death warrant. Why? For lack of a better answer, let us say they were made of a peculiar kind of stuff and could not do otherwise.

Whether there are any mystic forces pushing men along a path from which there is no escape, is a moot question. But there is no questioning the fact that throughout history men have regularly made excursions in quest of freedom, and that every one of these excursions was identified by its leadership. It is a logical inference therefore that when men of that stripe appear on the scene the cause of freedom is not neglected. Perhaps, after all, the present plight of free-dom in America is due to lack of leadership.

If, for instance, those who prate about "free enterprise" were willing to risk bankruptcy for it, even as the men of the Declaration risked their necks for independence, the present drive for the collectivization of capital would not

115

have such easy going. Assuming that they are fully aware of the implications of the phrase they mouth, and are sincere in their protestations, the fact that they are unwilling to suffer mortification of the flesh disqualifies them for leadership, and the case for "free enterprise" is hopeless.

The present low estate of freedom in this country must be laid to lack of the proper leadership—to men who know what freedom is and who do not equate it with their own "standard of living." Whether or not leadership could have averted, or can still stop, the trend toward socialism, may be open to question; that a glorious fight for freedom might yet enliven the American scene is not. Whether a fight for freedom will be crowned with success, is less important than the fight itself, for if nothing comes of it, the improvement in the spirit of the fighters will be a gain, and they cannot help but keep alive the values that will make America a better climate for their offspring to live in.

There is no accounting for the emergence of these superior men, these "sports of nature," who sporadically shape the course of mankind. They come, as it were, from nowhere, and nobody has yet conclusively explained their advent. But, they come. When in her own time and her own pleasure Nature deems America ready for and worthy of them, she will give us the men who will make the good fight. It seems reasonable to assume that their first objective will be— Repeal of the Sixteenth Amendment.

116

9 781258 047863